JAMESTOWN 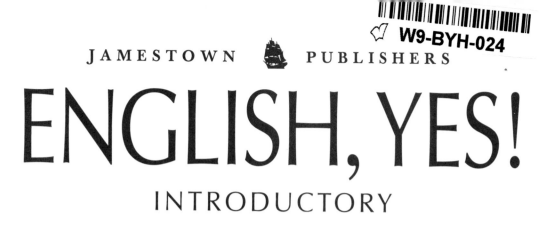 PUBLISHERS

ENGLISH, YES!

INTRODUCTORY

Learning English Through Literature

JAMESTOWN  PUBLISHERS

a division of NTC/CONTEMPORARY PUBLISHING GROUP
Lincolnwood, Illinois USA

W9-BYH-024

"Hello, Goodbye" by John Lennon/Paul McCartney,
© 1967, Paul McCartney,
Renewed 1995 Sony/ATV Songs LLC.
Administered by EMI Blackwood Music Inc. (BMI)

Original cover and interior design: Michael Kelly
Cover illustration: Westlight / © Jim Zuckerman

ISBN: 0-89061-915-8

Published by Jamestown Publishers,
a division of NTC/Contemporary Publishing Group, Inc.,
4255 West Touhy Avenue,
Lincolnwood (Chicago), Illinois 60712-1975 U.S.A.
© 1998 NTC/Contemporary Publishing Group, Inc.
All rights reserved. No part of this book may be reproduced,
stored in a retrieval system, or transmitted in any form or by any means,
electronic, mechanical, photocopying, recording, or otherwise,
without prior permission of the publisher.
Manufactured in the United States of America.
00 01 02 03 04 VH 12 11 10 9 8 7 6 5

Contents

JAMESTOWN PUBLISHERS

ENGLISH, YES!

INTRODUCTORY

Learning English Through Literature

HELLO, GOOD-BYE

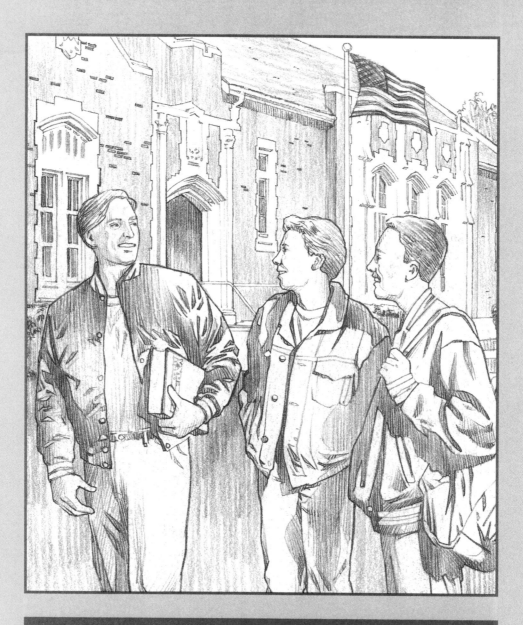

How do you say *hello* to a family member?
How do you say hello to a friend?
How do you say hello to a stranger?

Good-bye to the Old, Hello to the New

Last month I was in my native country. I said **good-bye** to
my grandparents, my cousins, and my friends. I was **sad.**
I was a little **worried** too. What about the future?

Now I live in a **different** country. I live in the United States.
5   I am in a different school. My sister is in a different
school too. We have **new** teachers and new friends. New
experiences are good!

I am **happy** here, but a new life isn't easy. Sometimes I
remember my grandparents in my country. Sometimes
10   I remember my **old** friends. Sometimes I am **lonely.**
Then I look at their pictures and I feel better. **Part of my
heart** is with them. And part of their heart is with me.

Hello, Good-bye

by John Lennon and Paul McCartney

You say **yes,** I say **no.**
You say **stop,** I say **go,** go, go.
Oh no!
You say good-bye and I say hello.
5   Hello, hello,
I don't know why you say good-bye.
I say hello.
Hello, hello,
I don't know why you say good-bye.
10   I say hello.

I say **high,** you say **low.**
You say why, and I say I don't know.
Oh no!
You say good-bye and I say hello.
15   Hello, hello,
I don't know why you say good-bye.
I say hello.
Hello, hello,
I don't know why you say good-bye.
20   I say hello.

YOU CAN ANSWER THESE QUESTIONS

Put an *x* in the box next to the correct answer.

Reading Comprehension

1. Last month the boy in the story was in
  ❏ a. the United States.
  ❏ b. his native country.

2. Now the boy is in
  ❏ a. the United States.
  ❏ b. his native country.

3. The boy said good-bye to his
  ❏ a. sister.
  ❏ b. grandparents.

4. In his new country, the boy is
  ❏ a. sad and worried.
  ❏ b. happy but some-times lonely.

5. In the song, the singer says *no.* Then the singer's friend says
  ❏ a. yes.
  ❏ b. no.

6. The singer and her friend think the same way.
  ❏ a. Right.
  ❏ b. Wrong.

Vocabulary

7. *Good-bye* and *hello* have
  ❏ a. the same meaning.
  ❏ b. different meanings.

8. When you are *worried,* you are
  ❏ a. not happy. You are thinking about your problems.
  ❏ b. tired. You are ready to go to bed.

Idioms

9. In the story, the boy says part of his heart is with his old friends. The idiom *part of my heart* means
  ❏ a. part of my body.
  ❏ b. part of my feelings and thoughts.

10. In the song, *Oh no* means
  ❏ a. there is a problem.
  ❏ b. there is not a problem.

How many questions did you answer correctly? Circle your score. Then fill in your score on the Score Chart on page 152.

Number Correct	1	2	3	4	5	6	7	8	9	10
Score	10	20	30	40	50	60	70	80	90	100

EXERCISES TO HELP YOU

Exercise A

Building sentences. Make sentences by adding the correct letter. One is done for you.

1. Last month I ____*c*____

2. I said good-bye _____

3. Sometimes I

   remember _____

4. Then I look _____

a. to my grandparents, my cousins, and my old friends.

b. my old friends.

c. was in my native country.

d. at their pictures.

Now write the sentences in the blanks below. Begin each sentence with a capital letter. End it with a period. One is done for you.

1. *Last month I was in my native country.*
2. _____
3. _____
4. _____

Do numbers 5–8 the same way. These sentences are about the song.

5. You say stop, and _____

6. You say good-bye _____

7. You say why _____

8. I don't know _____

a. why you say good-bye.

b. I say go, go, go.

c. and I say hello.

d. and I say I don't know.

5. _____
6. _____
7. _____
8. _____

Exercise B

Understanding the story. Answer each question. Complete the sentence. Look back at the story. One is done for you.

1. Where was the boy last month?

   Last month he was in his native country .

2. Who did the boy say good-bye to?

   He said good-bye .

3. The boy said good-bye. How did he feel?

   He was .

4. Where is the boy now?

   He is .

5. Is the boy in the same school or in a different school?

   He is .

6. How does the boy feel here in his new country?

   He is .

7. Who does the boy remember?

   He remembers .

8. What does the boy look at?

   He looks at .

Exercise C

Using the verb *be* correctly. Study this chart.

The Verb *Be:* Simple Present	
Singular	**Plural**
I am	We are
You are	You are
He is	They are
She is	
It is	

Fill in each blank. Use the present tense of the verb *be*. One is done for you.

1. The boy said good-bye.

   Now he _____is_____ in a new country.

2. The boy said good-bye to his grandparents.

   They _____ in the boy's native country.

3. The boy said, "I _____ happy in my new country."

4. The boy's sister is in the United States too.

   But she _____ in a different school.

5. The boy said, "We _____ in new schools."

6. The boy has new friends.

   They _____ in the United States.

7. The boy is happy in the United States.

   But sometimes he _____ lonely.

8. The boy remembers his old friends.

   They _____ a part of his heart.

Exercise D

Understanding vocabulary. *Opposites* are words with different meanings. For example, *happy* and *sad* are opposites. Complete the crossword puzzle.

Look at each clue. Find the opposite in the box. Write the opposite in the puzzle. One is done for you: 1 Across is *yes*. The opposite of *yes* is *no*.

happy hello high new no old part sad same stop yes

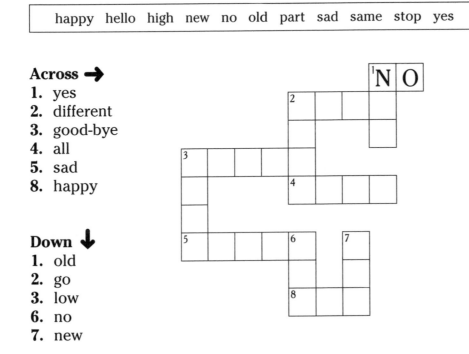

Across ➡

1. yes
2. different
3. good-bye
4. all
5. sad
8. happy

Down ⬇

1. old
2. go
3. low
6. no
7. new

Exercise E

Using vocabulary. Complete each sentence. Use a word from the box in Exercise D. Use each word once.

1. You said yes, and I said yes. We said the _____ thing.

2. I said yes, and you said _____. We said different things.

3. I am happy when I say hello. But sometimes I am _____ when I say good-bye.

4. I have many _____ friends in my native country, but I have many new friends here.

Understanding vocabulary. Some words in the story tell about the boy's feelings. Fill in the chart. Use the feeling words in the box.

happy	sad	worried	lonely

"Good Feelings"	"Bad Feelings"

Exercise G

Putting words in the correct order. Make sentences by putting the words in the correct order. Write each sentence in the blank. The sentences are about the story. One is done for you.

1. friends / good-bye / I / my / to / said

   I said good-bye to my friends   .

2. United States / I / in / the / live

   _____.

3. am / I / in / different / a / school

   _____.

4. new / friends / We / have

   _____.

5. remember / I / old / friends / my

   _____.

6. pictures / look / I / their / at

   _____.

Speaking up. Look at the conversation. Practice with two other students.

SHARING WITH OTHERS

Activity A
Choral reading. Work in two groups. Read the song on page 3.

Group 1 reads the first three lines.
Group 2 reads the next three lines.
Group 1 reads the next three lines.
Everybody reads the last line together.

Activity B
Sharing ideas. It's fun to share ideas with others. Discuss these questions with your partner or with the group. Write your answer to one of the questions.

How do you feel when you say hello to someone new?
How do you feel when you say good-bye to your family or friends?

_____

_____

_____

_____

_____

ROOTS

What are *roots?*
How do roots help plants grow?

Like a plant, each person has roots.
What are your roots?
How are your roots part of you?

Not Just Blue

"What is wrong?" Chi-Yin's mother asked. She **loved** her son very much. She saw that he was not happy.

"Nothing," Chi-Yin said. He picked up his **glass** and drank. The glass was **blue.** When he looked through it, everything
5   was blue.

"Something is wrong. You are sad," said his mother.

"Mother, what does **weird** mean?"

"I know this word in English," said his mother. "It means 'strange' or 'different.'" She smiled just a little.

10   "Some kids at school say that I am weird. They say I am not American," said Chi-Yin.

Chi-Yin's mother **twisted** the kitchen **towel** in her hands. "They are **right** and they are wrong. You were not born here. You are Chinese. But you are not weird." Chi-Yin
15   looked at his mother. He sighed.

"You are a very **special** boy. Your country has a great history. Be **proud** of your roots."

"Mother, I don't want to be different." Chi-Yin picked up his glass and looked through it. Everything was blue again.

20 "The world is interesting because people are different. Remember that, my son." Chi-Yin's mother took the glass from the **table.** "Be proud of who you are and where you come from. Because you are different, you are special."

Chi-Yin sat at the table in **silence.** He thought about his 25 mother's words. "I will remember, Mother. I'll **try hard to** remember."

Chi-Yin smiled. "It was like colors," he thought. "A **rainbow** of different colors was more **beautiful** than a rainbow of just blue."

YOU CAN ANSWER THESE QUESTIONS

Put an x in the box next to the correct answer.

Reading Comprehension

1. The two people in the story are
   ❏ a. a mother and a son.
   ❏ b. a father and a daughter.

2. At the beginning of the story, Chi-Yin was
   ❏ a. happy.
   ❏ b. sad.

3. Children at school told Chi-Yin that he was
   ❏ a. weird.
   ❏ b. special.

4. Chi-Yin was born in
   ❏ a. the United States.
   ❏ b. China.

5. Chi-Yin's mother said that it was good to be
   ❏ a. different.
   ❏ b. sad.

6. The story teaches you that it is good when
   ❏ a. everyone is alike.
   ❏ b. people are different.

Vocabulary

7. The mother told the boy that he was special. *Special* means
   ❏ a. not like everyone else.
   ❏ b. like everyone else.

8. When you are *proud* of your roots, you are
   ❏ a. pleased with where you come from.
   ❏ b. worried about where you come from.

Idioms

9. *What is wrong?* means
   ❏ a. What is the problem?
   ❏ b. What is the right answer?

10. The boy said he would try hard to remember his roots. The expression *try hard to* means
    ❏ a. do your best.
    ❏ b. forget to do some-thing.

How many questions did you answer correctly? Circle your score. Then fill in your score on the Score Chart on page 152.

Number Correct	1	2	3	4	5	6	7	8	9	10
Score	10	20	30	40	50	60	70	80	90	100

Exercise A

Building sentences. Make sentences by adding the correct letter.

1. The mother _____

2. She saw that her _____

3. She asked _____

4. The children said that _____

a. Chi-Yin was weird.
b. what was wrong.
c. loved her son.
d. son was sad.

Now write the sentences on the lines below. Begin each sentence with a capital letter. End it with a period.

1. _____

2. _____

3. _____

4. _____

Now do numbers 5–8 the same way.

5. Chi-Yin was _____

6. His country _____

7. Chi-Yin did not want _____

8. Because Chi-Yin is different, _____

a. has a great history.
b. he is special.
c. born in China.
d. to be different.

5. _____

6. _____

7. _____

8. _____

Exercise B

Understanding the story. Answer each question. Complete the sentence. Look back at the story.

1. What is the boy's name?

   His name _____.

2. Who was the boy with?

   The boy was with _____.

3. How did the boy feel at first?

   He felt _____.

4. What did the children call Chi-Yin?

   They called _____.

5. Where was Chi-Yin born?

   He _____.

6. What did the mother tell her son to be proud of?

   The mother told her son to be _____.

7. Why is the boy special?

   The boy is special _____.

8. Why is a rainbow beautiful?

   A rainbow is beautiful because it has _____.

Exercise C
Using pronouns correctly. Study this chart.

Subject Pronouns	
Singular	**Plural**
I	we
you	you
he	they
she	
it	

Fill in the blank. Use the correct subject pronoun. One is done for you.

1. The mother asked, "What is wrong?"

    _____*she*_____ saw that her son was not happy.

2. The son said nothing was wrong.

    _____ didn't want to talk about the problem.

3. The mother and boy talked together.

    _____ talked about the problem.

4. The kids at school said things to the boy.

    _____ said that he was weird.

5. The mother said to her son, "_____ are special."

6. The mother said, "You and I come from a great country.

    _____ are Chinese."

7. The boy said, "_____ don't want to be different."

8. The boy thought about what his mother said.

    _____ smiled.

Exercise D

Using past tense verbs correctly. Study this chart.

Past Tense
talk + ed   = talked
sigh + ed   = sighed
smile + ed = smiled

Fill in the blank with the past tense. Use the verb in parentheses ( ).

1. The mother _____ what was wrong. (ask)

2. The mother _____ her son very much. (love)

3. The boy _____ through the glass. (look)

4. The boy _____ to his mother's words. (listen)

5. The boy _____ at the end of the story. (smile)

Exercise E

Understanding irregular past tense verbs. The past tense of some verbs does not end in *-ed*. These are irregular verbs.

Verb	Past Tense
take	took

Look at the story. Find the past tense of each verb. Complete the verb.

Past Tense

1. see   _ _ w
2. drink   _ _ a _ _
3. say   _ a _ _
4. sit   _ _ _
5. think   t _ _ _ g _ _

Exercise F

Using past tense verbs correctly. Complete the sentences. Use the past tense of the verbs in Exercise E. Use each verb once.

1. Yesterday the boy _____ milk.

2. He _____ at the table.

3. He _____ about the kids at school.

4. He _____ that the world was blue through the glass.

5. He _____, "I'll try to remember my roots."

Exercise G

Understanding vocabulary. Read the words in the box. Write the words in the correct place in the chart. Some are done for you.

beautiful	blue	glass	happy	sad	table	towel

Things	Words that Describe People or Things
glass	beautiful

Exercise H

Using vocabulary. Correct the sentences about the story. Use the words in the chart in Exercise G.

1. The glass was ~~sad~~ *blue*.
2. The boy was happy.
3. A rainbow of many colors is weird.
4. The boy sat at the towel.
5. The boy picked up the table.
6. The mother twisted the glass.

Speaking up. Look at the conversation and then practice with a partner.

SHARING WITH OTHERS

Activity A

Acting out the story. Work with a partner. Act out the conversation between Chi-Yin and his mother.
1. Read the words in the quotation marks; for example: "What is wrong?"
2. Perform the actions.
3. Share your acting with the group.

Activity B

Sharing ideas. It's fun to share ideas with others. Discuss these questions with your partner or with the group. Write your answer to one of the questions.

What country do you come from?
What do you know about the history of your country?

Is it easy or hard to move to a new country?
Is it easy or hard to make friends with people from the new country?

_____

_____

_____

LIONS' TALES

Fables are very old stories.
People began to tell them many years ago.
Fables are usually about animals.

These stories teach us lessons about life.

What are some of the animals in fables?
Do you know any fables?

The Lion and the Rabbit

Fable 1

One day a **hungry** lion saw a rabbit. The rabbit was asleep. The lion wanted to eat the rabbit.

"This rabbit isn't very **big,**" said the lion to himself. "And I am very hungry." Then the lion saw something move
5   among the trees in the **forest.** It was a deer. "Yes!" thought the lion. "A deer is bigger than a rabbit. I will eat the deer."

The deer saw the lion. The deer began to run through the forest. It crashed through the trees and bushes and made a lot of **noise.** The noise woke up the rabbit. It ran away.

10   The lion ran after the deer. He tried to **catch** the deer, but the deer was very **fast.** It **escaped.**

"Now I am really hungry," thought the lion. "I will go back and eat that rabbit." When the lion **returned,** the rabbit was gone. "Now I have no food at all," **roared** the very
15   unhappy and very hungry lion.

Moral: Be happy with the things you have and don't be **greedy** for more.

The Mouse and the Lion

Fable 2

1   One day a mouse woke up a sleeping lion. The **angry** lion decided to eat the mouse.

"Please don't eat me," said the mouse. "You are the king of the jungle. Have mercy on me!"

5   "It's true," said the lion. "A good king **shows mercy.** You can go. I won't eat you."

"Thank you, king. I promise I will help you when you are **in trouble,**" said the happy mouse. The lion laughed.

A few days later hunters captured the lion. They tied him
10   to a tree with a strong, thick rope. The mouse heard the roar of the lion. He came to the tree. "Oh, king," said the mouse. "I am here to help you."

Lion said, "How can a **little** mouse help a **mighty** lion?"

"You'll see," said the mouse. He chewed the rope with his
15   teeth. Soon the rope broke, and the lion was **free.**

The mouse said, "Even a little mouse can **keep a promise** and **repay a favor.**"

Moral: Be nice to everyone. You may need help one day.

You can answer these questions

Put an x in the box next to the correct answer.

Reading Comprehension

1. In Fable 1, the lion first wanted to eat a
   - ❏ a. deer.
   - ❏ b. rabbit.

2. The lion decided to eat the deer because
   - ❏ a. the deer was bigger.
   - ❏ b. a rabbit can run faster than a deer.

3. In the end, the lion ate
   - ❏ a. the rabbit.
   - ❏ b. nothing.

4. In Fable 2, the lion was angry because the mouse
   - ❏ a. woke him up.
   - ❏ b. talked too much.

5. The mouse asked the lion
   - ❏ a. to free him.
   - ❏ b. not to eat him.

6. The mouse helped the lion. The mouse
   - ❏ a. freed the lion from ropes.
   - ❏ b. gave the lion food.

Vocabulary

7. Fable 1 teaches us not to be greedy. The word *greedy* means
   - ❏ a. very hungry.
   - ❏ b. always wanting more.

8. The lion tried to catch the deer, but the deer escaped. The word *escape* means
   - ❏ a. get free.
   - ❏ b. run fast.

Idioms

9. When you *keep a promise*, you
   - ❏ a. forget to do something.
   - ❏ b. do what you said.

10. When you *repay a favor*, you
   - ❏ a. help someone who helped you.
   - ❏ b. give someone money.

How many questions did you answer correctly? Circle your score. Then fill in your score on the Score Chart on page 152.

Number Correct	1	2	3	4	5	6	7	8	9	10
Score	10	20	30	40	50	60	70	80	90	100

Exercise A
Building sentences. Make sentences by adding the correct letter.

1. The lion wanted to _____   **a.** but the deer escaped.
                                  b. eat a rabbit.
2. A deer is bigger _____   **c.** the rabbit was gone.
                                  d. than a rabbit.
3. The lion tried to catch

   a deer, _____

4. When the lion returned, _____

Now write the sentences on the lines below. Begin each sentence with a capital letter. End it with a period.

1. _____
2. _____
3. _____
4. _____

Now do numbers 5–8 the same way. The sentences are about Fable 2.

5. The angry lion   **a.** lion to have mercy.
                                b. help the lion.
   decided _____   **c.** and the lion was free.
                                d. to eat the mouse.
6. The mouse asked the _____

7. The mouse promised to _____

8. The mouse chewed the rope, _____

5. _____
6. _____
7. _____
8. _____

Understanding the story. Answer each question. Write a
complete sentence. Look back at the stories.

Fable 1

1. How did the lion feel at the start of the story?

   He was very _____.

2. What animal did the lion see first?

   He saw _____.

3. What animal ran fast and escaped?

   _____ *ran fast and* _____.

4. How did the lion feel at the end of the story?

   He was very _____ *and very* _____.

Fable 2

5. Who woke the sleeping lion?

   _____.

6. Who captured the lion?

   _____.

7. What did the mouse hear?

   He heard _____.

8. How did the mouse help the lion?

   _____.

Exercise C

Using future tense verbs correctly. Study this chart.

Future Tense
will + verb
will + go = will go
I will go.
It will run.
We will read.

Fill in each blank in the story. Use the future tense of the verb in parentheses ( ). The first one is done for you.

The lion thought, "I am hungry. I ___*will eat*___ (eat) the
                                          1
rabbit." The lion saw a deer. "The deer is bigger than a rabbit.

So I _____ (catch) the deer." But the deer escaped. The
        2
lion was now very hungry. He thought, "I _____ (go)
                                              3
back, and I _____ (eat) the rabbit." When the lion
              4
returned, the rabbit was gone. The lion was unhappy. "Now I

_____ (have) no food at all," the lion thought.
      5

Exercise D

Adding an adjective. Adjectives are words that tell about people or animals. The words in the box are adjectives.

angry	fast	greedy	hungry	little	mighty

Complete each sentence. Use the correct word from the box.

Fable 1

1. The lion chased the deer because he was _____.

2. The deer was very _____, and it escaped.

3. Because the lion was _____, he had no food to eat.

Fable 2

4. The lion was _____ when the mouse woke him up.

5. The _____ lion was king of the jungle.

6. The lion was big, and the mouse was _____.

Exercise E

Putting words in the correct order. Make sentences by putting the words in the correct order. Write each sentence in the blank. The sentences are about Fable 2.

1. lion / captured / the / Hunters

   _____.

2. roared / anger / lion / The / with

   _____.

3. rope / mouse / chewed / The / his / teeth / the / with

   _____.

4. lion / free / was / The

   _____.

5. to / Be / nice / everyone

   _____.

Exercise F

Adding vocabulary. On the left are six words from Fable 1. Complete each sentence by adding the correct word.

catch   1. The lion saw the deer in the _____.
             He saw it move among the trees.

escaped   2. The lion ran after the deer. He tried
             to _____ it.

forest   3. The deer ran fast. It _____.

noise   4. The _____ woke up the rabbit.
             It went away.

returned   5. When the lion _____, the rabbit
             was gone.

roared   6. The lion _____ because it was very
             unhappy and very hungry.

Exercise G

Understanding idioms. Make idioms. Find the words that go together. Write the correct letter in the blank. The idioms are all in Fable 2. One is done for you.

1. keep ___*d*___   **a.** the favor

2. in _____   **b.** trouble

3. show _____   **c.** mercy

4. repay _____   **d.** a promise

Exercise H

Using idioms. Complete the sentences. Use the idioms from Exercise G. Use each phrase once.

1. The lion decided not to eat the mouse. He decided to

   _____ to the mouse.

2. The mouse promised to help the lion. He promised

   to _____.

3. Hunters captured the lion. The lion was tied to a tree. The

   lion was _____.

4. The mouse helped the lion. The mouse was able

   to _____. He did what he said.

Exercise I

Speaking up. Look at the conversation. Practice it with a partner.

Activity A

Pantomiming a fable. Work in groups. Act out one of the fables.
1. Choose which fable to act out.
2. Make a mask for each character in the story: Draw a face on paper. Tape the face to a stick.
     Story 1 characters: Lion, rabbit, deer
     Story 2 characters: Lion, mouse, two hunters
3. One person reads the fable. The others use the masks to show the action.
4. Take turns reading the fable.

Activity B

Reading fables. Work in small groups. Find a fable. Aesop's fables are good to use.
1. Read the fable together.
2. Talk about what happens in the fable. Talk about what the fable teaches about life.
3. Retell the fable to the class.
Be sure to tell these things:
     Tell about the characters. These are the animals or people in the story.
     Tell what happens at the beginning.
     Tell the important things that happen in the story.
     Tell what happens at the end.
     Tell what the fable teaches.

Activity C

Sharing ideas. It's fun to share ideas with others. Discuss these questions with your partner or with the group. Write your answer to one of the questions.

Which of the two fables do you like better? Why?

What did the lion do wrong in the first fable?
What did the lion learn in the second fable?
How are the two lions like people?

Do you know any fables with animals? Tell one of them.
What does the fable teach?

_____

_____

THE GREEN-EYED MONSTER

In English-speaking cultures, green can mean envy or *jealousy,* red can mean anger or danger, and yellow can mean fear or cowardice.

Do these colors mean the same thing in your culture? What do these colors mean to you?

The Green-Eyed Monster

John Lake left the house at seven o'clock. He waved good-bye to his **wife,** Lisa.

"Good-bye, darling," said Lisa. "Have a **safe** trip."

"Don't worry. I'll be back tomorrow night," said John.

5 John got into his **car** and **drove** away.

Lisa looked down at her hands. The sun made her wedding ring shine. Lisa sighed. She was not happy.

"John loves someone else," said Lisa. "I want to see the woman he loves." Lisa decided to **follow** John in her car.

10 John stopped his car a block from the house. He wasn't on a **business trip.** He was worried about Lisa. "Lisa loves someone else," he thought. "Will Lisa leave the house? Will she go and see someone else?" he wondered. Soon John saw Lisa drive by in her car. He followed her.

¹⁵ John saw Lisa **pass** him. "She is driving very fast," he thought. "I will hurry through the **alley** and **catch up with** her car."

Lisa couldn't see John's car. She decided to turn around and go through the alley. She **pressed** down on the
²⁰ **accelerator** with her foot.

Suddenly, John and Lisa saw each other. They were both driving very fast. They couldn't stop. Their cars **crashed** into each other. Everything **went black.**

In the **hospital,** two tired doctors talked. "It is very
²⁵ sad," said one doctor. "My **patient died.** His name was John. Before he died, he said, 'Please tell my wife that I love her.'"

"That is strange," said the other doctor. "My patient whispered, 'Tell my **husband** that I love him.' Then she died."

³⁰ "Well, the night is over for us."

"Yes," said the younger doctor. "I'm going home to my wife. Nights like this give me the **blues,** and she can always cheer me up."

YOU CAN ANSWER THESE QUESTIONS

Put an *x* in the box next to the correct answer.

Reading Comprehension

1. Lisa was John's
   - ❑ a. mother.
   - ❑ b. wife.

2. Lisa thought that John
   - ❑ a. loved someone else.
   - ❑ b. worked too hard.

3. John wasn't going on a business trip. He wanted to
   - ❑ a. see another woman.
   - ❑ b. follow Lisa.

4. Lisa drove fast. She wanted to
   - ❑ a. find John's car.
   - ❑ b. catch a train.

5. At the end of the story,
   - ❑ a. John died but Lisa lived.
   - ❑ b. both John and Lisa died.

6. John and Lisa really loved each other.
   - ❑ a. Right.
   - ❑ b. Wrong.

Vocabulary

7. John's and Lisa's cars crashed. *Crash* means
   - ❑ a. to hit one another.
   - ❑ b. to go off the road.

Idioms

8. John wanted to catch up with Lisa's car. The idiom *catch up with* means
   - ❑ a. capture something and hold it.
   - ❑ b. come from behind and get near something.

9. John's and Lisa's cars crashed. Everything went black. The idiom *went black* means that
   - ❑ a. night came, and it was dark.
   - ❑ b. John and Lisa did not know what was happening around them.

10. The night was over for the doctors. The idiom *be over* means
    - ❑ a. come to an end.
    - ❑ b. start again.

How many questions did you answer correctly? Circle your score. Then fill in your score on the Score Chart on page 152.

Number Correct	1	2	3	4	5	6	7	8	9	10
Score	10	20	30	40	50	60	70	80	90	100

EXERCISES TO HELP YOU

Exercise A
Building sentences. Make sentences by adding the correct letter.

1. John waved good-bye _____
2. John got _____
3. Lisa decided to _____
4. John stopped his car _____

   a. follow John.
   b. to his wife.
   c. a block from his house.
   d. into his car.

Now write the sentences on the lines below. Begin each sentence with a capital letter. End it with a period.

1. _____

2. _____

3. _____

4. _____

Now do numbers 5–8 the same way.

5. Lisa wanted to _____
6. Lisa and John were _____
7. Their cars _____
8. John said to tell his wife _____

   a. crashed.
   b. driving very fast.
   c. that he loved her.
   d. find John's car.

5. _____

6. _____

7. _____

8. _____

Exercise B

Understanding the story. Answer each question. Write
complete sentences. Look back at the story.

1. When did John leave the house?

   He left _____.

2. To whom did John wave good-bye?

   He waved _____.

3. What did Lisa decide to do?

   She decided _____ *in her car* .

4. John saw Lisa drive by. What did John decide to do?

   He decided to _____.

5. What place did they both drive through?

   They both drove _____.

6. What happened to their cars?

   Their cars _____.

7. Who said that she loved her husband?

   _____.

8. What happened to John and Lisa at the end?

   They both _____.

Exercise C
Using pronouns correctly. Study this chart.

Object Pronouns	
Singular	**Plural**
me	us
you	you
him	them
her	
it	

Fill in the blank. Use the correct object pronoun. One is done for you.

1. John said good-bye to his wife.

   He waved to _____*her*_____.

2. John got into his car.

   Lisa looked at _____ as he left.

3. "John loves someone else. He no longer loves _____," said Lisa.

4. John thought that Lisa loved someone else.

   He thought that she no longer loved _____.

5. John wanted to see where Lisa went.

   He decided to follow _____.

6. John and Lisa were in the hospital.

   The doctors tried to help _____.

7. John said, "Tell my wife that I love _____."

8. Lisa said, "Tell my husband that I love _____."

Exercise D
Studying irregular past tense verbs. Look at Unit 2, pages 18 and 19. Study the past tense verbs.

Here are more irregular verbs. Look at the story. Find the past tense of each verb. Complete the verb.

		Past Tense
1.	leave	_ _ f _
2.	get	_ _ _
3.	drive	_ _ _ v _
4.	go	_ _ _ t
5	think	_ _ _ _ _ _ _
6.	see	_ _ _

Exercise E
Using past tense verbs. Write about the story. Use past tense verbs. Some are regular, and some are irregular.

Follow this example:

John / **wave** good-bye to Lisa
John waved good-bye to Lisa.

1. John / **get** into his car.

   _____.

2. John / **drive** away.

   _____.

3. Lisa / **think,** "John loves someone else."

   _____.

4. Lisa / **decide** to follow John.

   _____.

5. Lisa and John / both **drive** very fast.

   _____.

6. They / **see** each other.

   _____.

7. Their cars / **crash** into each other.

   _____.

8. John and Lisa / **die** in the hospital.

   _____.

Exercise F

Adding vocabulary. On the left are six words from the story. Complete each sentence by adding the correct word.

alley

crashed

hospital

patients

pressed

safe

1. John was going away. Lisa said, "Have a _____ trip."

2. Lisa wanted to find John's car. So she went through the _____.

3. Lisa _____ down on the car's accelerator. She wanted to go fast.

4. John's and Lisa's cars _____.

5. John and Lisa were _____ in the hospital.

6. The doctors in the _____ tried to help them.

Exercise G

Speaking up. Look at the conversations. Practice them with a partner.

Activity A

Making a news report. Work in groups of three. Make a news report. Tell the story of the car crash in the story.
Here are roles you can play in the news report:

News reporter at TV desk in TV studio
News reporter at hospital
One of the doctors

Answer these questions in your news report:
1. Who were the people in the crash?
2. Where did the crash take place?
3. Where were the couple when they died?
4. What did they say before they died?

Activity B

Sharing ideas. It's fun to share ideas with others. Discuss these questions with your partner or with the group. Write your answer to one of the questions.

What do you think the story teaches? Here are some ideas to talk about:

It is good to tell your feelings to others.
It is not good to be jealous. Jealousy is a "green-eyed monster." It can make people do foolish things.

Here are some more English idioms with colors. What do you think they mean?

I'm excited. **My mom gave me the green light** to have a birthday party.
I didn't feel like going out, so I told **a white lie.** I said I had a headache.
I didn't expect to get a letter from Linda. It came **out of the blue.**

Do you know any other idioms with colors? What are they? What do they mean?

_____

_____

_____

_____

_____

THE GIFT

When do you give gifts?
When do you *receive* gifts?

What kinds of gifts do you like to get?
Who do you give gifts to?

The Gift

Cassie **had on** her best dress. To tell the truth, it was her only dress. She and her mother and four brothers were new to the neighborhood. They moved to the neighborhood only two weeks ago.

5 Cassie's family had very little money. Cassie usually wore her brothers' old clothes. She was happy that she liked old, **faded T-shirts** and **jeans.**

Yesterday her mother told her about an invitation. A neighbor had invited Cassie to a birthday party. Now
10 Cassie was in her dress, standing in front of a strange door. She rang the doorbell.

"Why, hello there!," said a **blond**-haired woman. "I'm Jeannie's mother. You must be Cassie, our new neighbor. Come on in." Cassie followed the woman through the
15 house into a **crowded** room. Balloons decorated the room. Cassie knew Jeannie from school. Cassie also **recognized** two or three other faces. They also were students at her high school. But most of the **guests** were **strangers** to her. "Hi, Cassie," said Jeannie. "Let me introduce you to
20 my friends."

Soon everyone gathered around the table with the gifts. Jeannie began to open her presents.

Everyone **clapped** as Jeannie opened each gift. She opened packages with CDs of **popular** singers. She opened
25 **attractive** bottles of perfume. Then she picked up Cassie's present. Cassie felt her **cheeks** turn **red.** She felt **dizzy.** Her head was spinning around.

Cassie's gift was in a simple **brown envelope.** Cassie thought it looked **ugly** and **cheap.** "What can this be?"
30 Jeannie asked.

Cassie said nothing. She felt sick to her **stomach.** How could her present ever compare to all those **expensive** gifts?

Jeannie slowly took a thick piece of paper out of the enve-
35 lope. "Oh," she said. "Look, everyone! Isn't it beautiful?"

Jeannie smiled and looked at Cassie. She held up a drawing of her own **face.** Cassie had made the picture the night before. "What a wonderful present from a special new friend!" exclaimed Jeannie.

Put an *x* in the box next to the correct answer.

Reading Comprehension

1. Cassie's family had
- ❑ a. a lot of money.
- ❑ b. very little money.

2. Cassie's family
- ❑ a. was new in the neighborhood.
- ❑ b. moved to the neighborhood two years ago.

3. Cassie went to the birthday party
- ❑ a. alone.
- ❑ b. with her brothers.

4. Jeannie received
- ❑ a. many expensive gifts.
- ❑ b. many T-shirts and jeans as gifts.

5. Cassie gave Jeannie
- ❑ a. an expensive gift.
- ❑ b. a gift she made herself.

6. Jeannie liked Cassie's gift.
- ❑ a. Right.
- ❑ b. Wrong.

Vocabulary

7. Cassie recognized only a few people at the party. The word *recognize* means
- ❑ a. know someone because you met the person before.
- ❑ b. look a lot like another person.

8. The room was crowded with guests. *Guests* are the people who
- ❑ a. give a party.
- ❑ b. come to a party.

9. The guests clapped as Jeannie opened each gift. The word *clap* means
- ❑ a. hit your hands together to show you like something.
- ❑ b. say what you think about something.

Idioms

10. Cassie *had on* her best dress. *Have on* means
- ❑ a. wear a piece of clothing.
- ❑ b. place something on top of something else.

How many questions did you answer correctly? Circle your score. Then fill in your score on the Score Chart on page 152.

Number Correct	1	2	3	4	5	6	7	8	9	10
Score	10	20	30	40	50	60	70	80	90	100

EXERCISES TO HELP YOU

Exercise A

Building sentences. Make sentences by adding the correct letter.

1. Cassie and her family

   were _____

2. A neighbor told Cassie's

   mother _____

3. Cassie knew Jeannie _____

4. Most of the guests _____

   a. from school.
   b. were strangers.
   c. about a birthday party.
   d. new to the neighborhood.

Now write the sentences on the lines below. Begin each sentence with a capital letter. End it with a period.

1. _____
2. _____
3. _____
4. _____

Now do numbers 5–8 the same way.

5. Jeannie began _____

6. Cassie felt her

   cheeks _____

7. Jeannie slowly took _____

8. Jeannie held _____

   a. up a drawing of her own face.
   b. a piece of paper out of the envelope.
   c. turn red.
   d. to open her gifts.

5. _____
6. _____
7. _____
8. _____

Exercise B

Understanding the story. Answer each question. Write complete sentences. Look back at the story.

1. When did Cassie's family move to the neighborhood?

   _They moved there_____._

2. What did Cassie like to wear?

   _She liked to wear_____._

3. Cassie received an invitation to a party. What kind of party was it?

   _It was a_____._

4. Who said hello to Cassie at the door?

   _____.

5. What gifts did Jeannie get?

   _She got_____._

6. Jeannie picked up Cassie's present. How did Cassie feel?

   _She felt_____._

7. What was Cassie's present?

   _Her present_____._

8. What did Jeannie do when she saw Cassie's gift?

   _Jeannie_____._

Exercise C

Using singular and plural nouns. Nouns in English can talk about one thing (singular) or two or more things (plural). Study this chart.

Plural nouns usually end in -s.

Singular	Plural
one girl	two girl**s**

Some nouns ending in s have plurals with -es.

Singular	Plural
one dress	three dress**es**

Complete each sentence. Use the singular or plural of the noun in parentheses ( ).

1. Cassie had many
   ___T-shirts___ (T-shirt).

2. Cassie had one
   _____ (dress).

3. There were many
   _____ (guest).

4. Cassie's gift was in an
   _____ (envelope).

Exercise D

Adding an adjective. Complete the sentences. Use the adjectives at the left. Read the words in dark type. They give clues to each adjective's meaning.

crowded   1. Cassie wore old, _____ jeans. The jeans **had lost their color.**

dizzy   2. The room was _____ with people. **There were many people there.**

expensive   3. Cassie thought that her gift looked _____. The other gifts were very attractive; her gift **did not look attractive.**

faded   4. Cassie saw that the other presents were _____. They **cost a lot of money.**

ugly   5. Cassie felt _____. **Her head was spinning.**

Exercise E

Using the verb *have* correctly. Study this chart.

The Verb *Have*	
Simple Present	
Singular	**Plural**
I have	We have
You have	You have
He has	They have
She has	
It has	

Fill in each blank. Use the present tense of the verb *have*. One is done for you.

1. Cassie _____*has*_____ four brothers.

2. She _____ only one dress.

3. Cassie's brothers _____ many T-shirts for her.

4. Cassie's mother said, "You _____ an invitation to a party."

5. Jeannie's mother said, "We _____ a new neighbor. Here's Cassie."

6. Jeannie _____ many friends.

7. Jeannie said, "I _____ a new friend."

8. People _____ birthdays once a year.

Exercise F

Describing clothes. Work with a partner. Look at the picture on page 41. Point to various people and tell what they have on.

Example: He has on jeans.

            They have on T-shirts.

Exercise G

Understanding vocabulary. The story has many words for parts of the body, for colors, and for clothes. Read the words in the box. Write the words in the correct place in the chart. Some are done for you.

blond brown cheek dress face hand jeans red stomach T-shirt

Parts of the Body	Colors	Clothes
cheek	blond	dress

Exercise H

Using vocabulary. Correct the sentences about the story. Use the words in the chart in Exercise G.

1. Cassie made a picture of Jeannie's ~~hand~~. *face*
2. Jeannie started to open the expensive gifts. Cassie's hands turned red.
3. Cassie's present was in a white envelope.
4. Jeannie's mother had red hair.
5. Cassie wore her jeans to the party.
6. Cassie wore dresses most of the time.

Exercise I

Speaking up. Look at the conversation. Practice it with a partner.

Activity A

Role-playing. Do this role-play with a partner. Each of you takes a turn.

You are Cassie. You come home from the party. Tell your mother or brothers what happened.

Use these ideas:

> Jeannie's mother met me at the door. She took me . . .
> There were many guests. I knew . . .
> Balloons decorated the room. There was a table . . .
> Jeannie opened many gifts. She opened . . .
> When Jeannie began to open my gift, I felt . . .
> When Jeannie saw my drawing, she . . .
> Now I feel . . .

Activity B

Sharing hobbies. Do you make things with your hands? What kinds of things do you make? Bring some things to class and tell about them.

Activity C

Sharing ideas. It's fun to share ideas with others. Discuss these questions with your partner or with the group. Write your answer to one of the questions.

What was the best gift you ever gave?
What was the best gift you ever received?

How do people celebrate birthdays in places you know?
Do they eat cake? Do they put candles on cake?
Do they give presents? What kind of presents do they give?

_____

_____

_____

_____

_____

CREATION STORIES

Every culture has a story that tells how the world began.
These stories are called creation stories.
Do you know a story about the beginning of the world?

Sumer: How the World Began

People in the land of Sumer told this story of how the world began. The people lived thousands of years ago in Asia.

In the beginning, all was chaos. **Wind** and **water** were everywhere. Everything was moving. Enlil, a god, decided to create a world from the chaos.

One god wanted to protect the chaos. This god **sent** a huge dragon to fight Enlil. The dragon was named Tiamat. Tiamat came with an army of dragons to stop Enlil.

Enlil asked the winds for help. When Tiamat began to fight, she **opened** her **enormous** mouth. Enlil forced all the winds inside the dragon's mouth. Tiamat swallowed the winds. She swelled up like a big balloon. She was so big that she could not move.

Enlil took a knife and **cut** her body into two pieces. He took one piece and put it down flat. This became the Earth. Then he took the other piece and made an **arch** over the **Earth.** This became the **sky.**

Next, the gods made humans. They cut off the head of Tiamat's husband. They mixed his **blood** with clay from the Earth. This is how the first humans **came to be.**

Finland: How the World Began

In ancient Finland, people told this story of how the world began.

In the beginning, there was only water. Above the water lived the goddess Air. Air had a daughter named Ilmatar.

Ilmatar liked to **explore** the waters. One day she traveled far. She decided to rest on the **surface** of the water.
5 Suddenly the wind started to blow strongly. **Waves** crashed around her. The storm lasted seven hundred years. After that, Ilmatar lived in the water.

One day Ilmatar was floating on her back. She bent one of her knees. A beautiful duck saw her knee. The duck
10 thought it was a hill and landed on it. There it laid seven **eggs.** The eggs became very hot. Ilmatar felt the heat from the eggs. She put her knee under the water to cool it. The eggs fell down to the bottom of the ocean.

Time passed. One of the eggs broke open. The **bottom** half
15 of the egg **shell** became the Earth. The **top** half of the shell became the sky. The yellow **yolk** of the egg formed the sun, and the white part became the moon and stars.

More time passed. Ilmatar had a baby named Vainamoinen. He swam in the water for seven years. He
20 then left the ocean and became the first human on Earth.

YOU CAN ANSWER THESE QUESTIONS

Put an *x* in the box next to the correct answer.

Reading Comprehension

1. In Story 1, the Earth came from a dragon's
   - ❑ a. body.
   - ❑ b. egg.

2. In Story 1, Enlil was
   - ❑ a. a god.
   - ❑ b. a dragon.

3. Enlil asked for help from the
   - ❑ a. waters.
   - ❑ b. winds.

4. In Story 2, the Earth came from a
   - ❑ a. goddess's body.
   - ❑ b. duck's egg.

5. Ilmatar was
   - ❑ a. a goddess's daughter.
   - ❑ b. the goddess Air.

6. Ilmatar's baby was the
   - ❑ a. first human.
   - ❑ b. first fish.

Vocabulary

7. The dragon's mouth was enormous. The word *enormous* means
   - ❑ a. big.
   - ❑ b. ugly.

8. Ilmatar liked to explore the waters. When you *explore,* you
   - ❑ a. forget where you are going.
   - ❑ b. go to new places.

9. The words *top* and *bottom*
   - ❑ a. are opposites.
   - ❑ b. are parts of an egg.

Idioms

10. Creation stories tell how things came to be. *Come to be* means
    - ❑ a. begin.
    - ❑ b. go someplace.

How many questions did you answer correctly? Circle your score. Then fill in your score on the Score Chart on page 152.

Number Correct	1	2	3	4	5	6	7	8	9	10
Score	10	20	30	40	50	60	70	80	90	100

EXERCISES TO HELP YOU

Exercise A

Building sentences. Make sentences by adding the correct letter.

1. Enlil decided _____

2. The dragon was _____

3. Enlil forced _____

4. Enlil cut the dragon's body _____

    a. into two pieces.
    b. named Tiamat.
    c. to create a world.
    d. the winds into the dragon's mouth.

Now write the sentences on the lines below. Begin each sentence with a capital letter. End it with a period.

1. _____

2. _____

3. _____

4. _____

Now do numbers 5–8 the same way.

5. Ilmatar liked to _____

6. A duck laid _____

7. One of the eggs _____

8. The top half of the eggshell _____

    a. broke open.
    b. explore the water.
    c. became the sky.
    d. seven eggs on her knee.

5. _____

6. _____

7. _____

8. _____

Exercise B
Understanding the story. Answer each question. Complete the sentences. Look back at the story.

Story 1

1. In the beginning, what was everywhere?

<u>*In the beginning*</u>   .

2. What did a god send to fight Enlil?

<u>*A god sent*</u>   .

3. What did Enlil force inside the dragon's mouth?

<u>*Enlil forced*</u>   .

4. What did Enlil cut into two pieces?

<u>*He cut*</u>   .

Story 2

1. After the storm, where did Ilmatar live?

<u>*After the storm, Ilmatar lived*</u>   .

2. How many eggs did the duck lay on Ilmatar's knee?

<u>*The duck laid*</u>   .

3. Where did the eggs fall?

<u>*The eggs fell down*</u>   .

4. What did the bottom half of one eggshell become?

<u>*The bottom half became*</u>   .

Exercise C

Using possessive nouns correctly. Possessive nouns in English end in *'s.* Possessive nouns tell about things that belong to someone.

Enlil's knife = Enlil has a knife; the knife belongs to Enlil

The dragon's enormous mouth = the dragon has an enormous mouth

Complete the story. Make a possessive noun from each word in parentheses ( ). Write the possessive in the blank.

1. The goddess Air had a daughter.

The _____ name was Ilmatar. (daughter)

2. Ilmatar decided to stay in the water.

The _____ home was the ocean. (woman)

3. The _____ eggs fell to the bottom of the ocean. (duck)

One became the Earth and sky.

4. Ilmatar had a baby.

The _____ name was Vainamoinen. (baby)

5. Vainamoinen left the sea.

The _____ home became the Earth. (child)

Exercise D

Adding prepositions. Here is a list of some of the prepositions in the story.

above	from	of	on	under

Complete the sentences by adding the correct preposition.

1. The goddess Air lived _____ the water.

2. Ilmatar bent one _____ her knees.

3. A duck landed _____ her knee.

4. Ilmatar felt the heat _____ the duck's eggs.

5. Ilmatar put her knee _____ the water to cool it.

Exercise E

Studying irregular past tense verbs. Find the past tense of these irregular verbs in the stories. Write them in the blanks.

1. send   _ _ _ _
2. cut   _ _ _
3. put   _ _ _
4. make   _ _ _ _
5. feel   _ _ _ _
6. fall   _ _ _ _
7. break   _ _ _ _ _
8. swim   _ _ _ _

Find the past tense of these verbs in the puzzle. Circle them. Note that some are regular and some are irregular.

ask
break
cut
decide
fall
feel
like
make
open
put
send
swallow
start
swim
want

M	A	D	E	B	P	W	M	P	V	S
S	E	N	T	W	U	A	L	R	Q	W
S	B	Z	C	U	T	N	Y	D	T	A
W	J	K	Y	H	P	T	F	E	L	L
A	S	K	E	D	M	E	C	C	B	L
M	R	O	S	Q	L	D	B	I	Z	O
X	K	D	O	P	E	N	E	D	F	W
B	R	O	K	E	J	K	E	E	W	E
J	N	S	T	A	R	T	E	D	Y	D
L	I	K	E	D	V	U	F	E	L	T

Exercise F

Using past tense verbs. Write four sentences about Story 1. Write about the dragon Tiamat. Use these verbs in the past.

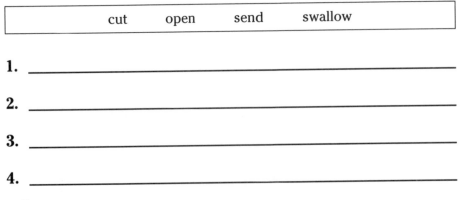

cut	open	send	swallow

1. _____

2. _____

3. _____

4. _____

Understanding vocabulary. Answer the riddles. Use the words in the box. Write the correct answer in the blank.

arch   blood   bottom   enormous   shell   surface   wave   yolk

1. I am the yellow part of an egg.

   What am I? _____

2. I am the opposite of top.

   What am I? _____

3. I am the hard, outside part of the egg.

   What am I? _____

4. I am red and I move through your body.

   What am I? _____

5. I mean the same as big.

   What am I? _____

6. I am round. I am like half of a circle.

   What am I? _____

7. I am in the ocean. I move on the surface of the water.

   What am I? _____

8. I am the top of things like the ocean or a table.

   What am I? _____

Exercise H

Speaking up. Look at the conversation. Practice it with a partner.

SHARING WITH OTHERS

Activity A

Telling the story in pictures. Draw three or four pictures to tell one of the creation stories. Use the stories in this book or other ones you know.

Here are some ideas:
>   Show what there was in the beginning.
>   Show how the world came to be.
>   Show how humans came to be.

Activity B

Sharing ideas. It's fun to share ideas with others. Discuss these questions with your partner or with the group. Write your answer to one of the questions.

What things are alike in the two stories?
What things are different?

Are these stories like other stories you know about creation? How are they different?

_____

_____

_____

_____

_____

_____

_____

_____

_____

_____

NAMES

How did you get your name?
Does it have a special meaning?

Was there a special *ceremony* or celebration when
you were born and named?

Names

"Some Russian names are very long, aren't they?" said the woman in the **university** admissions office. I just smiled.

"Call me Jackie," I said suddenly. "It's easier." I had **filled out** many **forms,** and I still had many more forms in front of me.

"I'm not able to fit your whole name into our computer," remarked the **clerk.** "Did you know that?"

"No, I didn't, but I am going to call myself Jackie," I said.

"Like Jackie Kennedy?" asked the clerk. "Did you pick the name because of her?" An image of the dead President's wife came into my mind. She had on an expensive French suit and a little round hat. If she was from Earth, I was from the moon. No, I didn't **choose** the name Jackie because of her. Will this clerk be able to understand my **choice?**

I closed my eyes and thought back to the last part of my long, long trip. In the **waiting area** for my last **flight,** there was an American family—a mother, a father, and their two children. The parents were reading **newspapers.** The little

20 girl was trying to read a book. Her brother kept putting his hand over the pages. Finally, the brother tried to **pull** the book away, and the girl **pushed** him hard.

"Jackie," cried the mother. "Shame on you! Behave!" I **expected** her to **scold** the boy, but it was to the girl that

25 she spoke. "Leave your brother alone!"

I smiled at the little girl. My eyes flashed the **message** "Life isn't **fair.**"

The girl looked at me and said, "One day I am going to do **exactly** what I want."

30 "I am too," I replied. "I am too."

YOU CAN ANSWER THESE QUESTIONS

Put an *x* in the box next to the correct answer.

Reading Comprehension

1. Jackie is a new
   - ❏ a. student from Russia.
   - ❏ b. teacher at the university.

2. Jackie's whole name is
   - ❏ a. very hard to say.
   - ❏ b. too long to fit in the computer.

3. Jackie picked her name because of
   - ❏ a. a little girl.
   - ❏ b. Jackie Kennedy.

4. The brother in the airport was being bad. The mother scolded
   - ❏ a. him.
   - ❏ b. the sister.

5. Jackie and the girl at the airport were alike. They both wanted to make their own choices.
   - ❏ a. Right.
   - ❏ b. Wrong.

6. Jackie Kennedy was
   - ❏ a. the wife of an American president.
   - ❏ b. the mother in the airport.

Vocabulary

7. The mother began to scold the girl. *Scold* means
   - ❏ a. tell someone that he or she is doing something wrong.
   - ❏ b. tell someone that you don't like him or her.

8. Jackie expected the mother to scold the boy, but the mother scolded the girl. *Expect* means
   - ❏ a. think that something will happen.
   - ❏ b. forget something important.

9. Jackie tried to tell the girl that "Life isn't fair." *Fair* means
   - ❏ a. the same for everyone; right or good.
   - ❏ b. happy and pleasant; with no problems.

Idioms

10. Jackie is filling out forms. *Fill out a form* means
    - ❏ a. write information on a form.
    - ❏ b. make something get bigger.

How many questions did you answer correctly? Circle your score. Then fill in your score on the Score Chart on page 152.

Number Correct	1	2	3	4	5	6	7	8	9	10
Score	10	20	30	40	50	60	70	80	90	100

Exercise A

Building sentences. Make sentences by adding
the correct letter.

1. Some Russian names _____

2. Jackie had filled _____

3. The woman is going to call

    _____

4. The woman didn't choose

    her name _____

    a. herself Jackie.
    b. because of Jackie Kennedy.
    c. are very long.
    d. out many forms.

Now write the sentences on the lines below. Begin each
sentence with a capital letter. End it with a period.

1. _____

2. _____

3. _____

4. _____

Now do numbers 5–8 the same way.

5. In the waiting area, there

    was an _____

6. The parents _____

7. The mother scolded _____

8. One day I am going to _____

    a. the little girl.
    b. do exactly what I want.
    c. American family.
    d. were reading a newspaper.

5. _____

6. _____

7. _____

8. _____

Exercise B

Understanding the story. Answer each question. Complete the sentences. Look back at the story.

1. Where did the first part of the story take place?

    It took place in _____ .

2. What did the Russian woman fill out?

    She filled out _____ .

3. What is the Russian woman going to call herself?

    She is going to _____ .

4. What did the woman see when she thought of Jackie Kennedy?

    She saw _____ .

5. Who did Jackie get her name from?

    She got her name from _____ .

6. Where did Jackie see the American family?

    She saw _____ .

7. What was the little girl trying to do?

    She was trying to _____ .

8. Who did the mother scold?

    She scolded _____ .

Exercise C

Using *be able to*. *Be able to* means the same as *can*.
I *can* speak Russian. = I *am able to* speak Russian.
Study this chart.

I am able to (swim).	We are able to (swim).
You are able to (swim).	You are able to (swim).
He is able to (swim). She is able to (swim). It is able to (swim).	They are able to (swim).

Complete the sentences about Jackie. Use *be able to*. Follow the example.

Example: speak English
        Jackie is able to speak English.

1. write in English

_____.

2. fill out forms in English

_____.

3. understand English

_____.

4. speak Russian

_____.

5. pick her own name

_____.

Write four things that you are able to do. Write four sentences.
You can use the ideas in the box. Or you can use your own ideas.

write in English   write with a computer   name ten U.S. presidents   sing well   swim   fill out forms in English

1. _____

2 _____

3. _____

4. _____

Exercise D

Using *be going to*. *Be going to means the same as* will.
I *will* name the baby Rita. = I *am going to* name the baby Rita.
Study this chart.

I am going to (eat).	We are going to (eat).
You are going to (eat).	You are going to (eat).
He is going to (eat). She is going to (eat). It is going to (eat).	They are going to (eat).

Complete the sentences about Jackie. Use *be going to*. One is done for you.

1. Jackie *is going to* study in the United States.

2. Jackie said, "I _____ call myself Jackie."

3. She _____ go to a big university.

4. Jackie _____ have classes every day.

5. She _____ make new friends.

6. Jackie said, "My friends _____ call me Jackie."

7. Jackie said, "We _____ do many things together."

8. She _____ do exactly what she wants.

Exercise E

Understanding vocabulary. Complete the crossword puzzle. Look at each clue. Find the correct word in the box. Write the word in the puzzle. One is done for you.

choose   expect   flight   form   pull   push   scold

Across
1. the opposite of *pull*
2. tell someone he or she is doing something wrong
5. a paper that you fill out with information
6. think that something will happen

Down
1. the opposite of *push*
3. take one thing instead of another
4. part of an airplane trip

Exercise F

Understanding vocabulary. Answer the riddles. Use the words in the box. Write the correct answer in the blank.

clerk   message   newspaper   university   waiting area

1. I am a kind of school. I come after high school. What am I?

   _____

2. I am a place to sit before a flight. What am I?

   _____

3. I work in an office. I fill out forms. What am I?

   _____

4. I am information you give to a person. What am I?

   _____

5. You read me. I am new every day. What am I?

   _____

Exercise G

Speaking up. Look at the conversations. Practice them with a partner.

SHARING WITH OTHERS

Activity A

Name research. Find a book about the meaning of names in English. Look up one or two names that interest you. What do they mean?
Share what you find in small groups.

Does your name have a special meaning? Share the meaning with your group.

Activity B

Sharing ideas. It's fun to share ideas with others. Discuss these questions with your partner or with the group. Write your answer to one of the questions.

Why did Jackie choose her name? What did her name mean to her?

You are able to choose another name for yourself. What name do you want to choose? Why?

_____

_____

_____

_____

ALL IN THE MIND

When bad things happen, do you *blame* yourself?
Or do you usually *blame* someone else?

Is it good or bad to blame someone else for things?

All in the Mind

Gerald threw back the covers and got out of bed.

Gerald looked at his wife. Her back was to him. She was sleeping. "Can't she **hear** that **music?**" he wondered. He left the bedroom. He knew that music. His son, Danny, had
5   played that song **over and over.** He and his son had even **argued** about it.

Now, every night for the last six months, Gerald heard that same music. Was he **going crazy?** During the day, he wasn't able to **concentrate** at work. **At night** he couldn't sleep
10   for more than a few minutes at a time.

Gerald went to the small window in the hall. Was there a radio outside? He looked out, but there was nothing to make noise. There were no cars on the street. There were no teenagers with radios. Gerald pressed his head against
15   the window glass. "Danny," he whispered.

Gerald closed his eyes. He could see everything happen again. It was like a video replaying the same thing over and over. The **accident** happened so quickly.

He was giving Danny a driving lesson. Danny drove too
fast around a **curve.** Gerald moved his foot over to the
pedals. He tried to reach the **brake,** but he pressed the
accelerator **instead.** The car went off the road and turned
over. Danny died, but Gerald lived.

Gerald remembered his wife's reaction to the news.
"My baby, you killed my baby. **Murderer!** I'll never **forgive**
you. Never!"

That was eight months ago. Now she looks at him with
empty eyes. She doesn't seem to hear the music.

Gerald **put on** his jeans and a T-shirt. He left the house
and started to walk. He closed his eyes. There was no
music now. His mind was **dark** and **quiet.** He never heard
the speeding car. He didn't see its lights. "Danny," he
cried as it hit him. "Danny," he whispered as he died.

Upstairs his wife heard the screeching **tires.** "An
accident," she thought. "Another family **torn apart.**" She
reached for the tiny tape player and moved it closer to
Gerald's pillow. He'd hear the music when he got back.
She'd **make sure** he'd never forget.

YOU CAN ANSWER THESE QUESTIONS

Put an *x* in the box next to the correct answer.

Reading Comprehension

1. Gerald heard music
- ❏ a. all day long.
- ❏ b. at night in bed.

2. Gerald's wife
- ❏ a. heard the music.
- ❏ b. didn't seem to hear the music.

3. Gerald's son, Danny,
- ❏ a. died in an accident.
- ❏ b. was in the hospital.

4. Gerald's wife called Gerald a
- ❏ a. murderer.
- ❏ b. bad driver.

5. At the end, Gerald
- ❏ a. went back to bed.
- ❏ b. died in an accident.

6. There was no music. Gerald was going crazy.
- ❏ a. Right.
- ❏ b. Wrong.

Vocabulary

7. Gerald and Danny argued about music. The word *argue* means
- ❏ a. fight with words.
- ❏ b. have the same ideas about.

8. Gerald was not able to concentrate at work. When you *concentrate,*
- ❏ a. you think about what you are doing.
- ❏ b. you forget what you are doing.

9. Gerald wanted to hit the brake, but he hit the accelerator instead. When you do something *instead,*
- ❏ a. you do the same thing twice.
- ❏ b. you do something different from what you first planned.

Idioms

10. Danny played the same song over and over. The idiom *over and over* means
- ❏ a. many times.
- ❏ b. one time.

How many questions did you answer correctly? Circle your score. Then fill in your score on the Score Chart on page 152.

Number Correct	1	2	3	4	5	6	7	8	9	10
Score	10	20	30	40	50	60	70	80	90	100

EXERCISES TO HELP YOU

Exercise A

Building sentences. Make sentences by adding the correct letter.

1. Gerald got out of _____   **a.** to concentrate at work.
                            b. bed.

2. Gerald wasn't able   **c.** music over and over.
                            d. happened very quickly.

    _____

3. Gerald heard the same

    _____

4. The accident _____

Now write the sentences on the lines below. Begin each sentence with a capital letter. End it with a period.

1. _____

2. _____

3. _____

4. _____

Now do numbers 5–8 the same way.

5. Danny drove too _____   **a.** the tiny tape player.
                            b. off the road.

6. The car went _____   **c.** fast around the curve.
                            d. his jeans and T-shirt.

7. Gerald put on _____

8. His wife reached for _____

5. _____

6. _____

7. _____

8. _____

Exercise B

Understanding the story. Answer each question.
Write complete sentences. Look back at the story.

1. Who was in the bedroom?

   _____.

2. Who was Danny?

   _____.

3. What did Gerald hear at night?

   He heard _____.

4. What did Gerald think was happening to him?

   He thought that he was _____.

5. Where did Danny drive too fast?

   Danny drove _____.

6. What did Gerald do at the end of the story?

   He _____.

7. What happened to Gerald at the end?

   _____.

8. Where did the music really come from?

   It came from _____.

Exercise C

Changing statements to questions. To make a question from a statement with the verb *be*, put the *be* verb first.

Study these examples:
There was a window in the hall.
Was there a window in the hall?
Gerald and his wife were in an accident.
Were Gerald and his wife in an accident?

Make these sentences into questions. Put a question mark (?) at the end of each question. One is done for you.

1. Gerald was in bed.

  Was Gerald in bed?

2. There was music in the bedroom.

  Was there

3. There was a radio outside.

  _____

4. There were cars on the street.

  _____

5. There were teenagers on the street.

  _____

6. Gerald was in the street at the end.

  _____

7. There was a tape player in the bed.

  _____

8. Gerald's wife was in bed at the end.

  _____

Work with a partner. Take turns. Ask each other the questions in Exercise C.

Examples:
A: Was there a window in the hall?
B: Yes, there was.

A: Were Gerald and his wife in an accident?
B: No, they weren't. Gerald and Danny were in an accident.

Exercise E

Adding prepositions. These prepositions are in the story.

about	around	at	during	for	on	out	off

Complete the sentences by adding the correct prepositions. Use each preposition once.

1. Gerald got _____ of bed.

2. Gerald looked _____ his wife.

3. Gerald and his son argued _____ a song.

4. Gerald was not able to concentrate _____ the day.

5. Danny drove too fast _____ a curve.

6. The car went _____ the road.

7. Gerald put _____ his jeans and T-shirt.

8. His wife reached _____ the tape player.

Exercise F

Understanding vocabulary. Match the words that go together to make phrases. Write the correct letter in the blank.

1. drive _____   **a.** sure

2. torn _____   **b.** night

3. heard _____   **c.** crazy

4. made _____   **d.** a car

5. at _____   **e.** apart

6. go _____   **f.** music

Exercise G

Using vocabulary. Complete the sentences. They tell about the story. Use the phrases from Exercise F. Use each phrase once.

1. Danny was learning to _____.

2. Gerald _____ in bed for the last six months.

3. Gerald couldn't sleep _____ because of the music.

4. "If I hear that music again, I'll _____," thought Gerald.

5. Upstairs his wife _____ the tape player was on.

6. The family was _____ because of the accident.

Exercise H

Speaking up. Look at the conversation. Practice it with a partner.

SHARING WITH OTHERS

Activity A
Retelling the story. Do a role-play. Be Gerald or his wife. Tell the story. Tell how you feel.

Example:
I am Gerald's wife. We had a son, Danny. We were a happy family. Then there was a car accident. My son, Danny, died. But I was angry.

Activity B
Sharing reading. What is your favorite part of the story? Read it to a partner.

Activity C
Sharing ideas. It's fun to share ideas with others. Discuss these questions with your partner or with the group. Write your answer to one of the questions.

Was Gerald a murderer? What do you think?

What did Gerald's wife do to him?
Was Gerald's wife a murderer? What do you think?

What kind of music do you like hear to over and over? What kind of music don't you like to hear over and over?

_____

_____

_____

_____

_____

_____

_____

_____

AN ANCIENT GREEK HERO

What is a *hero?*
What does someone do to be a hero?

What do you know about ancient Greece?
Do you know any stories about Greek heroes?

Perseus

Once a king named Acrisius asked a prophet about the future. The prophet said, "One day your baby grandson, Perseus, is going to kill you."

So Acrisius put Perseus and Perseus's mother, Danae, into
5   a large box. He put the box into the ocean. The waves carried the box to the island of Seriphus. There Perseus **grew up** into a **brave young** man.

Now, the king of Seriphus wanted to marry Danae. Perseus was against the marriage. So the king thought of a plan to
10 **get rid of** Perseus. The king asked Perseus to kill a **terrible** monster called Medusa. The brave Perseus accepted the king's **challenge.**

Medusa was once a beautiful woman with **long, lovely** hair. But she made the gods angry. She said that she was
15 more beautiful than the goddesses. So the gods **punished** her. They made her into a monster with **snakes** for hair. Medusa had a strange power. When anyone looked at her, that person **turned into** stone.

The gods decided to help Perseus. They gave him a **shiny**
20 shield and a sword.

After a long journey, Perseus arrived at Medusa's island. "How can I find the monster?" he asked. "I have to be careful. I can't look at her, or I will turn into stone." He **thought of** a plan. He listened for the sound of the snakes in her hair. Finally, he heard their hiss. He was near the monster!

"Now what do I do? I can't look at her to kill her." Then he noticed the sun shine off his shield. He could use the shield like a **mirror!** He could see Medusa in the shield without really looking at her. He went near the sleeping monster and cut off her head with the sword.

Perseus returned home with Medusa's head. The king of Seriphus accidentally looked at the head, and he turned into stone.

What happened to Perseus's grandfather? One day Perseus **took part in** some games. He threw a discus. The wind caught the discus. It hit an old man and killed him. The man was Acrisius.

So in the end, the prophet's words were true. We can't escape our **fate.**

You can answer these questions

Put an *x* in the box next to the correct answer.

1. Acrisius was worried that
   - ❏ a. he was going to grow old.
   - ❏ b. his grandson, Perseus, was going to kill him.

2. The king of Seriphus wanted to
   - ❏ a. look at a monster.
   - ❏ b. marry Perseus's mother.

3. Medusa said that she was
   - ❏ a. stronger than the goddesses.
   - ❏ b. more beautiful than the goddesses.

4. Medusa was able to change people into
   - ❏ a. snakes.
   - ❏ b. stone.

5. Perseus used his shield
   - ❏ a. to see Medusa.
   - ❏ b. to sleep on.

6. In the end, Perseus killed his grandfather.
   - ❏ a. Right.
   - ❏ b. Wrong.

Vocabulary
7. The gods punished Medusa. The word *punish* means
   - ❏ a. make a person ugly.
   - ❏ b. hurt someone because the person did something wrong.

8. The brave Perseus accepted the king's challenge. The word *challenge* means
   - ❏ a. ask someone to do something hard.
   - ❏ b. ask someone to do something to make money.

9. We can't escape our fate. The word *fate* means
   - ❏ a. what is going to happen to us.
   - ❏ b. the anger of the gods.

Idioms
10. Perseus thought of a plan to find Medusa. When you *think of* a plan, you
    - ❏ a. get an idea.
    - ❏ b. think something is right.

How many questions did you answer correctly? Circle your score. Then fill in your score on the Score Chart on page 152.

Number Correct	1	2	3	4	5	6	7	8	9	10
Score	10	20	30	40	50	60	70	80	90	100

EXERCISES TO HELP YOU

Exercise A

Building sentences. Make sentences by adding the correct letter.

1. The king asked a prophet

   _____

2. Perseus grew _____

3. A king asked Perseus to _____

4. The brave Perseus accepted _____

   a. the king's challenge.
   b. kill a monster.
   c. up into a brave young man.
   d. about the future.

Now write the sentences on the lines below. Begin each sentence with a capital letter. End it with a period.

1. _____

2. _____

3. _____

4. _____

Now do numbers 5–8 the same way.

5. Perseus thought _____

6. Perseus listened for

   _____

7. Perseus used his shield _____

8. We can't _____

   a. the sound of the snakes in Medusa's hair.
   b. escape our fate.
   c. of a plan.
   d. like a mirror.

5. _____

6. _____

7. _____

8. _____

Exercise B
Understanding the story. Answer each question.
Write complete sentences. Look back at the story.

1. Who was Perseus's grandfather?

   _____.

2. Where did the waves take Perseus and Danae?

   The waves took _____.

3. Who did the king of Seriphus want to marry?

   He wanted to _____.

4. What did the king ask Perseus to do?

   He asked Perseus to _____.

5. How did Medusa look?

   She was _____.

6. What power did Medusa have?

   She turned people _____.

7. Perseus was near Medusa. What did he hear?

   He heard _____.

8. How did Perseus kill Medusa?

   He cut _____.

Exercise C
Using possessives correctly. Study this chart.

Possessive Adjectives	
my	our
your	your
his	their
her	
its	

Fill in the blank. Use the correct possessive adjective. One is done for you.

1. The king was named Acrisius.

   _____*His*_____ grandson was named Perseus.

2. Danae had a son. _____ son was named Perseus.

3. Danae said, "Perseus and I came to an island.

   The island became _____ home."

4. The king told Perseus, "I want to marry

   _____ mother."

5. Perseus said to himself, "I don't want the king to marry

   _____ mother."

6. Medusa was once beautiful.

   She was proud of _____ hair.

7. Perseus listened for the snakes.

   Soon he heard _____ hiss.

8. Perseus thought of a plan.

   He thought, "I can use _____ shield as a mirror."

9. Perseus cut off Medusa's head. He used

   _____ sword.

10. The story says that we can't escape _____ fate.

Exercise D

Adding an adjective. Complete the sentences by adding the correct adjective. Use each adjective once.

brave

long, lovely

shiny

terrible

young

1. King Acrisius had a _____ grandson named Perseus.

2. Perseus accepted the king's challenge. He was _____.

3. Medusa's hair was once _____ and _____.

4. Medusa became a _____ monster.

5. The gods gave Perseus a _____ shield.

Exercise E

Putting words in the correct order. Make sentences by putting the words in the correct order. Write each sentence in the blank.

1. king's / accepted / Perseus / the / challenge

   _____.

2. king / asked / monster / kill / to / The /a / Perseus

   _____.

3. decided / to / help / The / gods / Perseus

   _____.

4. snakes'/ hiss / Perseus / heard / the

   _____.

5. Perseus / home / head / Medusa's / returned / with

   _____.

Exercise F

Understanding vocabulary. Many times verbs go together with other words to make phrases. Study the verb phrases at the left. Match them with their meanings. Write the correct letter in the blank.

1. grew up _____

2. got rid of _____

3. turned into _____

4. thought of _____

5. took part in _____

a. changed from one thing into another

b. became an adult; was no longer a child

c. had a new idea

d. did something with others; joined in

e. made someone or something go away

Exercise G

Using vocabulary. Complete the sentences with the phrases from Exercise F. Use each phrase once.

1. King Acrisius _____ Perseus. The king put him in a box and put the box on the ocean.

2. Perseus _____ on the island of Seriphus. The baby Perseus became a man.

3. People looked at Medusa, and they _____ stone.

4. Perseus _____ a plan to find Medusa.

5. Perseus _____ some games. He threw the discus.

Exercise H

Speaking up. Look at the conversations. Practice them with a partner.

SHARING WITH OTHERS

Activity A
Putting the story in order. Do this activity.

1. Choose five sentences from the story.
2. Write each sentence down on a separate piece of paper.
3. Work with a partner. Give your partner your sentences.
4. Put the sentences you have in order. Put the sentence that happened first in the story first. Put the sentence that happened second in the story next. Continue in this way.
5. Check your partner's sentences. Are they in the correct order?

Activity B
Sharing ideas. It's fun to share ideas with others. Discuss these questions with your partner or with the group. Write your answer to one of the questions.

Which words do you think describe Perseus?

brave
smart
stupid
foolish

Do you think that Perseus is a hero? Why or why not?

Do you think we can escape our fate? Why or why not?

_____

_____

_____

_____

_____

_____

_____

STICKS AND STONES

There is a saying, "Sticks and stones may break my bones, but words will never hurt me."
What do you think this means?

Can words hurt people? How?

Sticks and Stones

Charlotte felt beautiful. She knew that she had a **pretty** face. Everyone said so. "Charlotte, what big, brown eyes you have," said Mrs. Hooper, her next-door neighbor.

Charlotte had not always felt **attractive.** When she was
5 a little girl, she didn't make friends easily at school. At home, she had a **secret imaginary** friend. Her friend was named Rita. Rita looked just like Charlotte.

Charlotte and Rita were best friends. They played together. They looked through the old magazines in the
10 attic. They **dressed up** in old clothes. Sometimes they used Grandma's pans and made cookies. Charlotte and Rita liked putting their cookies into a picnic basket. Then they hid in a **closet** and ate them all.

As Charlotte grew up, Rita **disappeared** from Charlotte's
15 life. Food became Charlotte's best friend.

When Charlotte was nineteen, her doctor said, "Your **heart** is **weak.** You have to lose 100 pounds. You have to **exercise.** You need to protect your heart."

Many times, Charlotte almost gave up. She wanted to eat
20 and eat. But she didn't. She **kept up** her **diet.**

Charlotte lost 80 pounds. She began to feel pretty. She began to be interested in things around her. She liked to go to an outdoor cafe. She enjoyed watching the people. She imagined their lives.

25 Sometimes Charlotte imagined things about herself. She **enjoyed** dreaming about the future. In her dreams, she saw a **handsome** man. He stopped at her table and asked, "May I sit with you?" He and Charlotte often met at the **cafe.** They slowly **fell in love.**

30 Suddenly a noise surprised Charlotte. She looked up. Several boys and girls were standing beside her table.

"Hey, lady, give us that table," said a boy. "You've had it long enough."

"Yes, you ate too much already," said a girl.

35 Charlotte got up. She felt **embarrassed.** She imagined that everyone was looking at her. She no longer felt pretty.

Charlotte hurried away from the cafe. With every step, she felt bigger and uglier. She wanted to eat and eat. And once, she thought she saw Rita, waiting in the shadows.

Put an *x* in the box next to the correct answer.

Reading Comprehension

1. Some of Charlotte's neighbors told her that she looked
   - ❑ a. ugly.
   - ❑ b. pretty.

2. Rita was Charlotte's
   - ❑ a. imaginary friend.
   - ❑ b. grandmother.

3. The doctor told Charlotte to
   - ❑ a. forget Rita.
   - ❑ b. lose weight.

4. After she lost weight, Charlotte began to
   - ❑ a. eat more.
   - ❑ b. be interested in the people around her.

5. The boys and girls asked Charlotte to give them
   - ❑ a. her table.
   - ❑ b. some food.

6. The boys and girls made Charlotte feel
   - ❑ a. good about herself.
   - ❑ b. bad about herself.

Vocabulary

7. The words *attractive* and *pretty* have
   - ❑ a. the same meaning.
   - ❑ b. different meanings.

8. When Charlotte grew up, Rita disappeared. The word *disappear* means
   - ❑ a. no longer exist.
   - ❑ b. become more important.

9. The boys and girls made Charlotte feel embarrassed. When you are *embarrassed,* you are
   - ❑ a. pleased and happy.
   - ❑ b. confused and ashamed.

Idioms

10. In her dreams, Charlotte and the young handsome man fall in love. *Fall in love* means
    - ❑ a. start to like someone very much.
    - ❑ b. hurt oneself by falling on the ground.

How many questions did you answer correctly? Circle your score. Then fill in your score on the Score Chart on page 152.

Number Correct	1	2	3	4	5	6	7	8	9	10
Score	10	20	30	40	50	60	70	80	90	100

EXERCISES TO HELP YOU

Exercise A

Building sentences. Make sentences by adding the correct letter.

1. Charlotte knew that _____   **a.** just like Charlotte.
                                          b. lose weight.
2. Rita looked _____   **c.** packing cookies into a picnic basket.
3. Charlotte and Rita   **d.** she had a pretty face.

    liked _____

4. The doctor told Charlotte to _____

Now write the sentences on the lines below. Begin each sentence with a capital letter. End it with a period.

1. _____

2. _____

3. _____

4. _____

Now do numbers 5–8 the same way.

5. Charlotte lost _____   **a.** felt pretty.
                                          b. eat and eat.
6. She enjoyed _____   **c.** 80 pounds.
                                          d. dreaming about the future.
7. At the end, she

    no longer _____

8. Charlotte wanted to _____

5. _____

6. _____

7. _____

8. _____

Exercise B

Understanding the story. Answer each question. Write complete sentences. Look back at the story.

1. At the start of the story, how did Charlotte feel?

She felt _____.

2. Who was Rita?

She was Charlotte's _____.

3. What did Charlotte and Rita do together?

They _____.

4. After Rita disappeared, what was Charlotte's best friend?

Her best friend _____.

5. Who told Charlotte to lose weight?

_____.

6. Who did Charlotte see in her dreams?

She saw _____.

7. What did the girl tell Charlotte?

She told Charlotte _____.

8. At the end of the story, how did Charlotte feel?

_____.

Exercise C
Using the verb *enjoy*. The verb *enjoy* means "like very much."
Another verb often comes after it. The second verb ends in *-ing*.

Study the verbs.

Charlotte *enjoyed eating.*
Charlotte *enjoyed watching* people.

Write sentences about Charlotte. Follow the example.

Example:
play with Rita   Charlotte enjoyed playing with Rita.

1. look through magazines

_____.

2. make cookies

_____.

3. eat cookies

_____.

4. go to an outdoor cafe

_____.

5. think about people's lives

_____.

6. think about her future

_____.

7. dream about a handsome man

_____.

Exercise D

Using the verb *like*. The verb *like* is often followed by another verb. Study the forms.

Charlotte *liked to eat.*   Charlotte *liked eating.*
Charlotte *liked to watch*   Charlotte *liked watching*
    people.   people.

Make two sentences about Charlotte using the verb *like*.

1. play with Rita

    a. _____.

    b. _____.

2. dream about her future

    a. _____.

    b. _____.

Exercise E

Review of *enjoy* and *like*. Write about things you like to do. Look in the box for ideas. Use the correct form.

read in English   play sports   go to cafes   watch TV   run   eat cookies

1. I enjoy _____.

2. I like to _____.

Exercise F

Using the verb *have to*. The verb *have to* tells about things you must do or need to do. The past tense of *have to* is *had to*.

Write about what Charlotte had to do. Follow the example.

Example:
lose weight   Charlotte had to lose weight.

1. eat less

_____.

2. exercise

_____.

3. make friends

_____.

4. talk to people

_____.

Exercise G

Understanding idioms with *up*. Many idioms in English have the word *up*. Match the idioms with their definitions. Write the correct letter in the blank.

1. dressed up _____   **a.** stopped doing something

2. grew up _____   **b.** was no longer a child; became an adult

3. gave up _____   **c.** wore good clothes

4. kept up _____   **d.** stood up; got to one's feet

5. got up _____   **e.** continued; opposite of stopped

Exercise H

Using idioms with *up*. Answer these questions about yourself.
1. Where did you grow up?

_____

2. When was the last time you dressed up?

_____

3. Did you ever promise yourself to lose weight or exercise? How long did you keep up your promise?

_____

4. Did you ever stop doing something? What did you give up?

_____

Exercise I

Speaking up. Look at the conversation. Practice it with a partner.

Sharing with Others

Activity A

Thinking of endings. Do this activity.

1. Discuss this question in groups:
   What will happen to Charlotte next?

Share your answers.

2. Give the story a happy ending.
   Work in groups and think of a happy ending. Ideas:
   When Charlotte is running away, she meets the handsome man of her dreams.
   Rita helps Charlotte lose more weight.

Share your happy ending with other groups.

Activity B

Retelling the story. Do a role-play. Be Charlotte.
Tell how you feel.

1. Tell how you feel when are sitting at the cafe table.
   I feel pretty and attractive. I lost 80 pounds. I enjoy . . .
2. Tell how you feel when you meet the boys and girls.
   I am surprised. People in the cafe usually don't talk to me.
   The boys and girls . . .
3. Tell how you feel after you leave the cafe.
   I no longer feel . . .

Activity C

Sharing ideas. It's fun to share ideas with others. Discuss these questions with your partner or with the group. Write your answer to one of the questions.

You read about the saying "Sticks and stones may break my bones, but names will never hurt me." Is the saying true for Charlotte?

How was Charlotte hurt by words?
Why does Rita appear at the end of the story?

What health problem does Charlotte have? What other kinds of health problems do people have? How can people end these problems?

_____

_____

_____

THE WORLD IS WRONG, NOT ME

Some people *complain* all the time. They are never happy.

Do you know someone who complains all the time?
Do you think people like this can change?

The Complainer

Every day Calvin Rogers gets up at seven o'clock. He makes coffee. Then he waits for the morning paper.

Yesterday Calvin was not happy. His newspaper was **late.** "Where is that **lazy** kid?" he thought. "When I see that
5   paperboy, I'll scold him."

Calvin sat down **slowly** on the porch swing. His left leg hurt him for the last three days. A light wind made the spring flowers move **gently** and send **sweet** smells into the air. The sun covered the stairs with yellow light. Calvin
10   didn't **notice.** "Fifteen minutes without my paper," Calvin thought. "Time wasted."

Calvin went inside his house. "I'm going to call the newspaper office and complain," he decided. "That kid should lose his job." Calvin went into the kitchen to get the phone
15   book. Then he remembered that it was upstairs. He had used it last night to find the number of the local radio station. He called to complain about the **loud** rock music.

Calvin was at the top of the stairs. His left leg suddenly **gave way**, and he fell backwards. He rolled down the
20   stairs. Calvin felt pain go through his body. Then he **blacked out.**

Calvin opened his eyes. He was at the bottom of the stairs. His leg was **bent** under him. It **hurt** terribly. "I have to call for help," he thought. "But who will hear me?"

25 Long minutes passed. Calvin saw the sunlight move into the house through the open front door. The light touched his **fingertips.** They **glowed** orange. "It's beautiful," he thought. "The color of peaches."

Suddenly a voice cried, "Mr. Rogers, what happened?"
30 Then he saw a woman's face. "Mr. Rogers, don't move."

Calvin tried to speak, but nothing came out. The woman ran into the kitchen and telephoned for help. Then she hurried back beside him. "Don't worry. Help is **on the way.**"

"Who are you?" Calvin asked weakly.

35 "I'm Timmy's mother. Timmy, your paperboy." She smiled at him. "I'm sorry I'm late. Timmy told me to be **on time.** He's at home **sick.**"

Calvin felt something turn inside him. His eyes filled with tears. "Thank you so much," he said. "You have a
40 **wonderful** boy."

YOU CAN ANSWER THESE QUESTIONS

Put an *x* in the box next to the correct answer.

Reading Comprehension

1. Yesterday Calvin was not happy because
 ❑ a. the newspaper was late.
 ❑ b. he lost his phone book.

2. Calvin likes to
 ❑ a. complain.
 ❑ b. enjoy flowers.

3. Calvin fell and broke
 ❑ a. his arm.
 ❑ b. his leg.

4. At the bottom of the stairs, Calvin began to notice
 ❑ a. the world around him.
 ❑ b. all the things wrong with his house.

5. The person who helped Calvin was the
 ❑ a. next-door neighbor.
 ❑ b. mother of the newspaper boy.

6. At the end, Calvin still wanted to complain.
 ❑ a. Right.
 ❑ b. Wrong.

Vocabulary

7. Calvin didn't notice the flowers. When you *notice* something, you,
 ❑ a. see, feel, or hear it.
 ❑ b. don't want to know about a problem.

8. Calvin's newspaper was late. Calvin wanted to call the newspaper office and complain. When you *complain,* you
 ❑ a. say you are not happy about something.
 ❑ b. say you are happy about something.

Idioms

9. The woman told Calvin that help was on the way. The idiom *on the way* means that something is
 ❑ a. going to happen soon.
 ❑ b. moving very fast.

10. The newspaper was not on time. The idiom *on time* means come
 ❑ a. before a certain time.
 ❑ b. at the right time.

How many questions did you answer correctly? Circle your score. Then fill in your score on the Score Chart on page 152.

Number Correct	1	2	3	4	5	6	7	8	9	10
Score	10	20	30	40	50	60	70	80	90	100

EXERCISES TO HELP YOU

Exercise A
Building sentences. Make sentences by adding the correct letter.

1. Every day Calvin waits

   _____

2. Calvin was _____

3. Calvin went into the kitchen

   to _____

4. Calvin rolled _____

a. down the stairs.
b. going to call the newspaper office.
c. for the morning paper.
d. get the phone book.

Now write the sentences on the lines below. Begin each sentence with a capital letter. End it with a period.

1. _____

2. _____

3. _____

4. _____

Now do numbers 5–8 the same way.

5. Calvin's leg _____

6. The sunlight _____

7. Calvin saw _____

8. Calvin told the woman that _____

a. touched his fingertips.
b. hurt terribly.
c. she had a wonderful boy.
d. a woman's face.

5. _____

6. _____

7. _____

8. _____

Exercise B

Understanding the story. Answer each question.
Write complete sentences. Look back at the story.

1. What time does Calvin get up every day?

    He gets up _____.

2. What was late yesterday?

    _____.

3. Why was Calvin going to call the newspaper office?

    He was going to call the newspaper office to _____.

4. What did Calvin complain about last night?

    He complained _____.

5. Calvin rolled down the stairs. What did he feel?

    _____.

6. Who helped Calvin?

    _____.

7. Who was Timmy?

    _____.

8. Where was Timmy?

    _____.

Using the present tense. Study this chart.

Simple Present Tense	
Singular	**Plural**
I run.	We run.
You run.	You run.
He runs.	They run.
She runs.	
It runs.	

Note the *-s.*

Calvin **waits** for the newspaper every day.

Complete the sentences. Use the present tense. Use the *-s* form. One is done for you.

1. Every day Calvin ____*sleeps*____ until seven o'clock. (sleep)

2. He _____ at seven o'clock. (get up)

3. He _____ down the stairs. (walk)

4. He _____ coffee. (make)

5. He _____ eggs. (eat)

6. He _____ for the newspaper. (wait)

7. He _____ the newspaper. (read)

8. He _____ to the radio. (listen)

Adding prepositions. Here is a list of some of the prepositions in the story.

about at for from inside of under without

Complete the sentences by adding the correct prepositions. Use each preposition once.

1. Calvin gets up _____ seven o'clock.

2. He waits _____ the paper.

3. Calvin was _____ his paper for fifteen minutes.

4. Calvin went _____ his house.

5. Calvin wanted to complain _____ the paperboy.

6. Calvin fell _____ the top of the stairs.

7. His leg was bent _____ him.

8. His skin was the color _____ peaches.

Exercise E

Understanding adjectives. Match each adjective with its meaning. Write the correct letter in the blank.

1. late _____   **a.** not feeling well

2. lazy _____   **b.** not on time; coming after the right time

3. sweet _____   **c.** not liking to work

4. loud _____   **d.** very good; very nice

5. sick _____   **e.** making a lot of noise

6. wonderful _____   **f.** having a nice taste or smell

Adding an adjective. Complete the sentences by adding an adjective. Use the adjectives from Exercise E. Use each adjective once.

1. At the start of the story, Calvin thought that the newspaper boy was _____.

2. Calvin was waiting for the newspaper. It was _____.

3. The flowers had a _____ smell. Calvin didn't notice it.

4. Calvin complained about the _____ music.

5. The newspaper boy was at home because he was _____.

6. At the end of the story, Calvin thought that the newspaper boy was _____.

Exercise G

Speaking up. Look at the conversations. Practice them with a partner.

SHARING WITH OTHERS

Activity A
Word game. Do this activity.

1. Work with a partner. Choose five words from the story.
2. Write a clue for each word.

Examples:
This is something people drink. You drink it from a cup.
(Answer: coffee)

This has the news. People read it every day.
(Answer: newspaper)

3. Work with other pairs. Give them your clues.
4. Write the words for the clues you have. How many words does your pair get right?

Activity B
Sharing ideas. It's fun to share ideas with others. Discuss these questions with your partner or with the group. Write your answer to one of the questions.

How did Calvin change at the end?
Do you think Calvin will complain in the future?

Is it good to complain? What do you think?

_____

_____

_____

_____

_____

_____

APPLES, APPLES

Nature gives us many wonderful fruits and vegetables to eat.
How many fruits and vegetables can you name?

What is your favorite fruit?

Mountain Mary

People in every country tell stories about their history. Sometimes they tell about heroes or other famous people. Here are two people who are famous in the United States.

*Both of these people lived about 200 years ago. Both loved nature. Both lived alone. Both left a **legacy** for future generations of people.*

Her real name was Maria Jung, but everyone called her Mountain Mary. She lived in Pennsylvania. She lived alone, but everyone in the area loved her. She was kind and **generous.** She especially **cared about** animals. She
5 **refused** to hurt them. When animals ate the plants in her garden, she caught them. But she didn't kill them. She took the animals up to the hills and set them free. Mountain Mary especially loved apples. She cut off parts of two apple trees and grew the parts together. This way
10 she **created** a new kind of apple known as the Good Mary. When she died in 1819, the local preacher told the people in his church there was one less **saint** on earth.

Johnny Appleseed

His real name was John Chapman, but people called him
Johnny Appleseed. He lived in the Ohio River valley.
He walked from place to place through the countryside.
He carried nothing but a tin **cup** and a **sack** of apple **seeds.**
5   He walked through the forests to small towns and farms.
He planted many apple seeds. This way people were able
to enjoy apples far into the future. He sometimes
exchanged small apple trees to get food and clothes for
himself. People in the area **treated** him with **respect.** He
10   was the man who loved apples.

Johnny Appleseed also loved animals. Once he saw that
moths were dying from the **heat** of his campfire. He didn't
want to kill them. He didn't like to hurt a living creature.
So he **put out** the fire. Because of this, he ate uncooked
15   food, and he was **cold** himself. He died in 1845, and the
kind of apple known as Johnny Weed was named for him.

Put an *x* in the box next to the correct answer.

Reading Comprehension

1. The stories about Mountain Mary and Johnny Appleseed
   - ❏ a. are true.
   - ❏ b. are not true.

2. Mountain Mary and Johnny Appleseed
   - ❏ a. lived in the past.
   - ❏ b. live today.

3. Both Mountain Mary and Johnny Appleseed loved nature.
   - ❏ a. Right.
   - ❏ b. Wrong.

4. Both Mountain Mary and Johnny Appleseed created a new kind of apple.
   - ❏ a. Right.
   - ❏ b. Wrong.

5. Both Mountain Mary and Johnny Appleseed moved from place to place.
   - ❏ a. Right.
   - ❏ b. Wrong.

Vocabulary

6. Mountain Mary and Johnny Appleseed left a legacy for future generations. A *legacy* is
   - ❏ a. something expensive.
   - ❏ b. something you give to your children or to younger people.

7. The word *generous* means
   - ❏ a. loving animals more than anything else.
   - ❏ b. liking to share or give things to others.

8. The preacher said there was one less saint. The word *saint* means
   - ❏ a. a good and holy person.
   - ❏ b. a person who works on a farm.

9. People respected Johnny Appleseed. When you *respect* someone, you show that you
   - ❏ a. have a good opinion about the person.
   - ❏ b. think the person needs money from you.

Idioms

10. The idiom *care about* means
    - ❏ a. like something or someone very much and want to help.
    - ❏ b. help grow a plant from when it is small.

How many questions did you answer correctly? Circle your score. Then fill in your score on the Score Chart on page 152.

Number Correct	1	2	3	4	5	6	7	8	9	10
Score	10	20	30	40	50	60	70	80	90	100

EXERCISES TO HELP YOU

Exercise A

Building sentences. Make sentences by adding the correct letter.

1. Mountain Mary _____

2. Mountain Mary cared

   _____

3. She refused _____

4. She created _____

   a. a new kind of apple.
   b. lived about two hundred years ago.
   c. to hurt animals.
   d. about animals.

Now write the sentences on the lines below. Begin each sentence with a capital letter. End it with a period.

1. _____

2. _____

3. _____

4. _____

Now do numbers 5–8 the same way.

5. Johnny Appleseed

   walked _____

6. He planted _____

7. People treated him _____

8. An apple _____

   a. from place to place.
   b. with respect.
   c. many apple seeds.
   d. was named for him.

5. _____

6. _____

7. _____

8. _____

Exercise B

Understanding the story. Answer each question. Write complete sentences. Look back at the stories.

1. When did the two people in the stories live?

   They lived _____.

2. Where did the two people in the stories live?

   _____.

3. What did the two people in the stories love?

   They loved _____.

4. What was Mountain Mary's real name?

   Her _____.

5. Where did Mary take the animals in her garden?

   She took _____.

6. Where did Johnny Appleseed walk?

   He walked _____.

7. What did Johnny Appleseed carry with him?

   He carried _____.

8. What did Johnny exchange to get food?

   He exchanged _____.

Exercise C

Using negatives in the past tense. Negative sentences are sentences with *not.* The contraction for *did not* is *didn't.*

Johnny Appleseed *didn't have* a house.
For verbs in the past tense, the negative uses *didn't.* The base form of the verb follows *didn't.*

Base Verb	Past Tense	Negative in the Past Tense
have	had	didn't have
live	lived	didn't live
eat	ate	didn't eat

Complete the sentences with negative verbs in the past. Use the verbs in parentheses ( ). One is done for you.

1. Mountain Mary *didn't live* in New York. (live)

   She lived in Pennsylvania.

2. Mountain Mary _____ to hurt animals. (want)

   She cared about animals.

3. She caught animals in her garden.

   But she _____ the animals. (kill)

4. She _____ a new kind of vegetable. (make)

   She created a new kind of apple.

5. Johnny Appleseed _____ many things. (carry)

   He carried only a cup and a sack.

6. Johnny _____ much money. (have)

   He exchanged apple trees to get food.

7. He saw moths near his campfire.

   He _____ to kill them. (want)

8. He put out his campfire.

   He _____ his food. (cook)

Studying past tense verbs. Find the past tense of the verbs at the left in the puzzle. Circle the past tense. Some verbs are regular, and some verbs are irregular.

call   grow
care   have
carry   leave
catch   live
cook   love
create   refuse
die   tell
eat   want

W	C	Q	L	E	F	T	C	P	A	C
C	A	R	R	I	E	D	R	X	D	A
A	U	G	C	O	O	K	E	D	I	R
L	G	R	E	W	W	L	A	O	E	E
L	H	B	H	A	D	O	T	M	D	D
E	T	N	Y	L	I	V	E	D	X	O
D	H	W	A	N	T	E	D	Z	P	A
U	S	V	T	O	L	D	M	N	Z	T
Q	R	E	F	U	S	E	D	F	W	E

Exercise E

Using the past tense. Complete the sentences. Use verbs from Exercise D.

1. Both Mountain Mary and Johnny Appleseed

   _____ during the early days of the United States.

2. Both Mountain Mary and Johnny Appleseed _____

   a legacy for future generations.

3. Both Mountain Mary and Johnny Appleseed _____

   nature.

4. Some animals _____ plants in Mary's garden.

5. Mary _____ the animals in her garden, but she

   didn't kill them.

6. She _____ to hurt a living creature.

7. She _____ parts of different apple trees together.

8. She _____ a new kind of apple.

9. The preacher _____ the people that Mary was a saint.

10. His real name was John Chapman, but everyone _____

    him Johnny Appleseed.

11. He _____ only a cup and sack.

12. He _____ in 1845.

Adding vocabulary. On the left are six words or idioms from the story. Complete each sentence by adding the correct word or idiom.

cared about

1. Johnny Appleseed and Mountain Mary left a _____. They left many plants to future generations. They also showed that nature is important.

hurt

2. Mary liked and helped people and animals. She _____ them.

generous

3. Mary helped people and animals. She was kind and _____.

legacy

4. People thought Johnny Appleseed was a good person. They treated him with _____.

put out

5. Johnny didn't want to _____ the moths near his campfire.

respect

6. So he _____ his fire.

Exercise G

Speaking up. Look at the conversation. Practice it with a partner.

Activity A

Making riddles. Follow the directions.

1. Work with a partner. Write 5 statements. Each tells about Mountain Mary, Johnny Appleseed, or both.

Examples:
I lived two hundred years ago. (Both)
I lived in the Ohio River valley. (Johnny Appleseed)
I had a garden. (Mountain Mary)

2. Work with another pair.

Read your clues to them. How many can they guess right? Then they read their clues to you. How many can you guess right?

Activity B

Sharing ideas. It's fun to share ideas with others. Discuss these questions with your partner or with the group. Write your answer to one of the questions.

What was the legacy of Mountain Mary?
What was the legacy of Johnny Appleseed?

Who are some famous people in the history of a country you know?
Why are these people famous?
Why do other people respect them?

_____

_____

_____

_____

_____

_____

HARVEST TIME

The *seasons* are a part of nature.
What is your favorite season?
What makes it special?

Harvest time is the time of year when people pick
food from fields. What seasons are harvest time?

How is human life like the seasons?

Harvest Time

Granny looked out at the fields filled with fruits and vegetables. She felt the **cool** night air through the open **kitchen** window. "It's time to start to **can**," she thought.

In her mind, she was already able to see the kitchen
5   shelves filled with shiny **jars** of peaches, pears, and plums. She could see jars filled with tomatoes, beets, and carrots. "Harvest time is the best time of year," thought Granny.

She looked out the window up into the night sky. There were many **stars.** They seemed unusually **bright.** Several
10   stars seemed to **move** in the sky. Granny finished cleaning the kitchen. The news was on the local radio station. "People continue to disappear from our area. Two more **are missing**. . . . We're in the middle of an unusually cool period for this time of year. . . . People report seeing
15   **strange** objects in the sky."

Granny really wasn't **paying attention.** She felt a cold breeze and closed the window.

Granny lived alone. Her husband was dead. Her children and grandchildren lived in the city. She slowly climbed
20   the **stairs** to bed. She was tired. She worked all day in the fields.

That night she had a dream. She saw all her family together in their Sunday clothes. They were having a picnic. They waved to her. "I'm happy to see you," she tried to say. But they disappeared into a great white **light.**

25

Suddenly Granny woke up. She remembered her dream. She noticed that her room was filled with a white light like in her dream. There was a humming noise like a machine. Her whole house was shaking.

30

Then she heard a loud sound above her. The **roof** of her bedroom disappeared. She heard the nails come out of the roof. Then a **force lifted** her up out of her bedroom. It pulled her up into the night sky. She was pulled up like any carrot ready for harvest, torn from its bed in the ground.

35

Granny **closed** her eyes tightly. Soon the noise stopped, and she felt herself **put down.** Granny slowly opened her eyes. She saw that she was in a kind of **container.** Through the glasslike walls of the container, she could see out. She saw other containers with moving **forms** in them. All were part of the harvest.

40

YOU CAN ANSWER THESE QUESTIONS

Put an *x* in the box next to the correct answer.

Reading Comprehension

1. Granny wanted to put fruits and vegetables
   - ❏ a. in jars.
   - ❏ b. in the refrigerator.

2. The radio said that
   - ❏ a. people were disappearing.
   - ❏ b. the harvest was bad that year.

3. Granny had a dream about
   - ❏ a. the harvest.
   - ❏ b. her family.

4. In her bed, Granny saw a light, and she heard
   - ❏ a. a crash.
   - ❏ b. a humming noise.

5. At the end, Granny was in a container in the sky.
   - ❏ a. Right.
   - ❏ b. Wrong.

6. What do you think happened?
   - ❏ a. Creatures from another world took Granny.
   - ❏ b. Someone played a trick on Granny.

Vocabulary

7. Granny could see the jars filled with tomatoes. The word *jar* means
   - ❏ a. a container made of glass.
   - ❏ b. something to drink from.

8. The force lifted Granny out of the bedroom. The word *lift* means
   - ❏ a. move up.
   - ❏ b. move down.

Idioms

9. Granny was not paying attention to the radio. When you *pay attention,* you
   - ❏ a. listen to and think about what is said.
   - ❏ b. do not listen to what is said.

10. People were missing from the area. The idiom *be missing* means
    - ❏ a. be moving.
    - ❏ b. be gone.

How many questions did you answer correctly? Circle your score. Then fill in your score on the Score Chart on page 152.

Number Correct	1	2	3	4	5	6	7	8	9	10
Score	10	20	30	40	50	60	70	80	90	100

Exercises to Help You

Exercise A
Building sentences. Make sentences by adding the correct letter.

1. Granny looked _____
2. In her mind, Granny could _____
3. Several stars seemed to _____
4. That night Granny _____

    a. had a dream.
    b. out at the fields.
    c. move in the sky.
    d. see jars filled with fruit.

Now write the sentences on the lines below. Begin each sentence with a capital letter. End it with a period.

1. _____
2. _____
3. _____
4. _____

Now do numbers 5–8 the same way.

5. Granny's room was _____
6. The roof of Granny's bedroom _____
7. A force lifted _____
8. Granny was in _____

    a. disappeared.
    b. filled with a white light.
    c. a container.
    d. Granny out of her bedroom.

5. _____
6. _____
7. _____
8. _____

Exercise B

Understanding the story. Answer each question.
Write complete sentences. Look back at the story.

1. Where was Granny at the start of the story?

   _____.

2. What time of the year was it?

   It _____.

3. What kinds of fruits and vegetables did Granny put into
   jars?

   Granny put _____.

4. What was strange about the sky?

   Several _____.

5. Who did Granny see in her dream?

   _____.

6. What disappeared from Granny's bedroom?

   _____.

7. Where did the force pull Granny?

   The force pulled Granny _____.

8. What did Granny see from her container?

   She saw _____.

Exercise C

Using contractions. A contraction is a short form. In a contraction, two words are used together. Study this chart.

Contractions with *Be*	
Present Tense	
Singular	**Plural**
I'm (= I am)	we're (= we are)
you're (= you are)	you're (= you are)
he's (= he is)	they're (= they are)
she's (= she is)	
it's (= it is)	

Complete the sentences. Use contractions with *be*. One is done for you.

1. Granny thought, "_____*It's*_____ time for the harvest."

2. The radio said, "_____ in the middle of a cool period."

3. Granny thought, "_____ tired."

4. Granny was tired.

   She thought, "_____ time for bed."

5. Granny saw her family in a dream.

   She thought, "_____ in their Sunday clothes."

6. Granny saw her husband in a dream.

   She thought, "_____ happy to see me."

7. Granny heard the strange noise.

   "_____ scared," she thought.

8. At the end, Granny is no longer at her home.

   _____ in a container in the sky.

Exercise D

Using *there was* and *there were*. A singular noun comes after *there was*. A plural noun comes after *there were*.

Singular
There was a strange noise.

Plural
There were many stars in the sky.

Complete the sentences with *There was* or *There were*. One is done for you.

1. _There were_ many vegetables in the fields.

2. _____ an old woman in the kitchen.

3. _____ shelves in the kitchen.

4. _____ many people in Granny's dream.

5. _____ a bright light in Granny's bedroom.

6. _____ a strong humming noise in Granny's bedroom.

7. _____ many containers in the sky.

8. _____ people in the other containers in the sky.

Exercise E

Understanding vocabulary. Look back in the story. Find the words for each category. Complete the words.

Fruits	Vegetables	Things in the House
p _ _ _ h e s	t _ m _ _ _ e s	k _ _ c h _ _
p _ _ r s	b _ _ t s	s t _ _ _ s
_ l _ m s	c _ _ _ _ t s	b _ d r _ _ m
		r _ _ f

Exercise F

Answer the riddles. Use the words from Exercise E. Write the correct answer in the blank.

1. I am red. I grow above the ground.

   What am I? _____

2. I am the top of a house. What am I? _____

3. You cook and make food in me. What am I? _____

4. You walk up me. What am I? _____

5. I am orange. I grow under the ground.

   What am I? _____

6. Sometimes my skin is green. You can eat me.

   What am I? _____

Exercise G

Speaking up. Look at the conversations. Practice them with a partner.

SHARING WITH OTHERS

Activity A
Telling the story in pictures. Draw pictures to show
the story.

1. Draw a picture of Granny at the beginning of the story.
2. Draw a picture of Granny at the end of the story.
3. Draw a picture of any other part of the story.

Talk about your pictures in small groups.

Activity B
Sharing ideas. It's fun to share ideas with others. Discuss
these questions with your partner or with the group. Write
your answer to one of the questions.

Who do you think took Granny into the sky?
What unusual things do you think were happening?

Do you think any part of the story was scary?
Which part? Why?

Stories about people from other planets are called science
fiction. Do you know any science fiction stories? Share them.

_____

_____

_____

_____

_____

_____

_____

_____

_____

GUILT AND GRASS

Part 1

What kinds of *chores* do you do around your house?
Do you like to do chores?

Do you know people who always talk about others?
Why do you think people say bad things about others?

Guilt and Grass

Part 1

Mrs. Farley and Mrs. King spent Thursday mornings together. They stood at the back **fence** between their **yards.** They met there about 8:45 a.m. They waited for Georgia Haney Graham to come out of her house in her
5   gardening clothes.

While they waited, they talked about their neighbors. They **gossiped** about their **neighbors'** problems. They talked about the Harrelson girl. "When are she and her boyfriend going to get married?" they asked. They
10   remarked about Mr. Jackson's new job. "Is he going to make enough money?" they asked. But most of all, they wondered about Georgia Haney Graham. "Why does she come out every Thursday to **mow** her **lawn?**" they asked. "She is seventy-five years old!"

15   Georgia put on her old straw hat. She left the cool **interior** of her house for the bright sun **outside.** She took the old lawn mower from the back **shed.** She noticed her neighbors already at the back fence. "Gossips," she said to herself. "The only thing they do is to talk about their
20   neighbors."

Georgia didn't like to be in the sun. But still she came out every Thursday to mow the lawn. She **struggled** to push the old lawn mower over the **grass.**

She knew that Mrs. Farley and Mrs. King wondered about
25   her. "They really want to know why I do this," she thought. Then she **frowned.** As she mowed, she thought back to the beginning.

It was the year the handsome young English teacher came to her high school. The usual English teacher, Mrs. Ryan,
30   had a car accident. The new teacher was going to **take her place** for the rest of the school year. All the girls wanted Mr. Wallace to notice them, and so did Georgia.

When Mr. Wallace **announced** a poetry **contest,** Georgia decided to be the winner. Every night after school, Georgia
35   tried to write a **poem.** But every night she got lost in a **daydream:** Mr. Wallace was giving her the first-place **prize,** and he looked deeply into her eyes. The days passed. Georgia had a drawer filled with crumpled papers. But she didn't have a poem. So what happened the day of the
40   contest seemed like fate.

To be continued.

YOU CAN ANSWER THESE QUESTIONS

Put an *x* in the box next to the correct answer.

Reading Comprehension

1. Georgia was
   - ❏ a. an old woman.
   - ❏ b. a young woman.

2. Every Thursday morning, Georgia
   - ❏ a. gossiped with her neighbors.
   - ❏ b. mowed the lawn.

3. Mrs. Farley and Mrs. King were
   - ❏ a. Georgia's friends.
   - ❏ b. Georgia's neighbors.

4. Mrs. Farley and Mrs. King wondered why Georgia
   - ❏ a. wasn't married.
   - ❏ b. mowed the lawn.

5. Georgia was
   - ❏ a. able to write a poem for the contest.
   - ❏ b. not able to write a poem for the contest.

Vocabulary

6. Mrs. Farley and Mrs. King gossiped about their neighbors. The word *gossip* means
   - ❏ a. talking about yourself.
   - ❏ b. talking about other people.

7. Georgia struggled to move the lawn mower over the grass. The word *struggle* means
   - ❏ a. work hard; make a big effort.
   - ❏ b. move like a snake.

8. Mr. Wallace announced a poetry contest. A *contest* is
   - ❏ a. a game or test that often has a prize.
   - ❏ b. a meeting at school where all students come.

9. Georgia daydreamed that she won the prize. The word *daydream* means
   - ❏ a. sleep during the day instead of at night.
   - ❏ b. think about some nice things that might happen.

Idioms

10. The idiom *take someone's place* means
   - ❏ a. do someone's job, often for a certain time.
   - ❏ b. move into someone's house for a certain time.

How many questions did you answer correctly? Circle your score. Then fill in your score on the Score Chart on page 152.

Number Correct	1	2	3	4	5	6	7	8	9	10
Score	10	20	30	40	50	60	70	80	90	100

EXERCISES TO HELP YOU

Exercise A

Building sentences. Make sentences by adding the correct letter.

1. Mrs. Farley and

    Mrs. King _____

2. Georgia came out every

    Thursday _____

3. Georgia struggled to push _____

4. The two women wondered _____

a. about Georgia.
b. the lawn mower over the grass.
c. to mow the lawn.
d. talked about their neighbors.

Now write the sentences on the lines below. Begin each sentence with a capital letter. End it with a period.

1. _____

2. _____

3. _____

4. _____

Now do numbers 5–8 the same way.

5. The new teacher

    took _____

6. Georgia decided to _____

7. Georgia _____

8. Georgia got lost _____

a. win the poetry contest.
b. Mrs. Ryan's place.
c. tried to write a poem.
d. in a daydream.

5. _____

6. _____

7. _____

8. _____

Exercise B
Understanding the story. Answer each question.
Write complete sentences. Look back at the story.

1. Where did Mrs. Farley and Mrs. King meet?

   They met _____.

2. Who did they wait for?

   They waited _____.

3. How old was Georgia?

   _____.

4. What did Georgia do every Thursday morning?

   She mowed _____.

5. Who was Mr. Wallace?

   _____.

6. What did Mr. Wallace announce?

   He announced _____.

7. What did Georgia decide to do?

   She decided _____.

8. What did Georgia see in her daydream?

   Mr. Wallace gave _____.

Exercise C
Using question words. Study this chart.

Who	for people:	*Who* mowed the lawn? *Georgia* mowed the lawn.
What	for things:	*What* did Georgia put on? Georgia put on *her old hat.*
When	for time:	*When* did the women meet? They met *in the morning.*
Where	for places:	*Where* was the mower? It was *in the shed.*
Why	for reasons:	*Why* did Georgia wear her hat? She wore it *because the sun was hot.*

Complete each question with the correct question word.

1. _____ did Mrs. Farley and Mrs. King stand?

   They stood **at the back fence.**

2. _____ did Mrs. Farley and Mrs. King meet?

   They met **about 8:45 A.M.**

3. _____ did Mrs. Farley and Mrs. King meet?

   They met **because they wanted to gossip.**

4. _____ did they wait for?

   They waited for **Georgia.**

5. _____ did Georgia take from the shed?

   She took **the old lawn mower** from the shed.

6. _____ didn't like to be in the sun?

   Georgia didn't like to be in the sun.

7. _____ did Georgia mow the lawn?

   She mowed the lawn **every Thursday.**

8. _____ did Georgia push?

   She pushed **the lawn mower.**

Exercise D

Putting words in the correct order. Make sentences by putting the words in the correct order. Write each sentence in the blank. The sentences are about the story.

1. women / talked / The / neighbors / about / their

   _____.

2. Georgia / old / hat / put / her / on

   _____.

3. took / mower / Georgia / from / shed / the / the

   _____.

4. noticed / Georgia / fence / at / neighbors / the / her

   _____.

5. like / Georgia / didn't / be / to / sun / the / in

   _____.

Exercise E

Understanding vocabulary. Match each word at the left with its meaning. Write the letter in the blank.

1. announced _____

2. fence _____

3. frowned _____

4. grass _____

5. mowed _____

6. prize _____

7. shed _____

8. yard _____

a. a small house to keep tools in
b. cut (the grass)
c. a green plant that covers a yard
d. a railing or wall, often made of wood, around a yard
e. told people news
f. area in front or in back of a house
g. looked unhappy or angry
h. something you get when you win a contest

Exercise F

Using vocabulary. Complete the sentences. The sentences tell about the story. Use the words from Exercise E. Use each word once.

1. The two women stood at the _____.

2. Georgia _____ the lawn on Thursday.

3. Georgia went out into the _____ behind her house.

4. Georgia's lawn mower was in the _____.

5. It was hard to cut the _____ with the old lawn mower.

6. Georgia _____ when she thought about the past. Her face showed that her thoughts were not happy.

7. The teacher _____ a poetry contest. There was going to be a prize.

8. Georgia had a daydream. In it, she was the winner of the poetry _____.

Exercise G

Speaking up. Look at the conversation. Practice them with a partner.

SHARING WITH OTHERS

Activity A
Guessing the end. What will happen next? What do you think Georgia's secret is?

1. Work in small groups. Think of two secrets.
2. Share your ideas with the class.

Activity B
Reading a poem. Follow these directions.
1. Look for a poem in English. Choose a poem you like. Practice reading it.
2. Read your poem to a small group.

Activity C
Sharing ideas. It's fun to share ideas with others. Discuss these questions with your partner or with the group. Write your answer to one of the questions.

What did Mrs. Farley and Mrs. King gossip about?
What did they want to know about Georgia?

What did Georgia think about Mrs. Farley and Mrs. King? Did she like them?

Were you ever in a contest? What happened?
Did you ever win a prize? What happened?

_____

_____

_____

_____

_____

_____

_____

GUILT AND GRASS

Part 2

Do you think it is wrong to *cheat* at school?
Why?

Did you ever find something another person lost?
Did you try to return it? What happened?

Why do you think people *steal*?

Guilt and Grass

Part 2

The day of the poetry contest, Georgia didn't eat lunch.
She went to sit at her **favorite** place in the park. There she
noticed a notebook. She opened it, but there was no name
in it. The notebook was filled with drawings and poems.
5   She **got interested in** looking at the drawings in the book.
Then she read one of the poems. After that, things seemed
to happen as in a dream.

Georgia's poem won first place in the contest. The **last** day
of the school year, she walked up to the stage in front of
10   the entire school. Mr. Wallace gave her the prize. When he
handed it to her, he looked deeply into her eyes. He said
that she surprised him with her **talent.** Georgia **received
congratulations** from all her family and friends. But she
didn't feel **happy.**

15   Summer was always Georgia's favorite time of year. But
that year she wasn't **looking forward to** it. She **rarely**
went to the swimming pool or on picnics with her friends.
She felt a shadow over her. She seemed to **always** be
carrying a great weight.

20　One hot morning she heard the sound of the lawn mower in the yard. The heat was already **terrible.** There was a young black man mowing the lawn. His shirt was wet with **sweat** from the heat. "That's not a job I would like. I'm glad my parents **hire** someone to do it," Georgia thought.

25　The man walked by her window. Georgia **realized** that she recognized him. His face was among those in the notebook.

"Would you like a glass of water?" Georgia asked when he went by the window again.

"Why yes, ma'am, thank you," said the young man. When 30　she handed him the glass, he looked **directly** at her. He studied her face with a **serious** look. He **hesitated** for a moment. Then he spoke. "I read about your poetry prize in the newspaper. Congratulations."

"Thank you," Georgia answered.

35　"You chose one of my favorite poems," he said. With that, he gave the mower a push and walked out of her **view.**

Georgia spent the rest of the summer inside. The next summer Georgia told her parents, "I'll take care of the yard work." And she **continued** to do so for the rest of her life.

You can answer these questions

Put an *x* in the box next to the correct answer.

Reading Comprehension

1. The day of the poetry contest, Georgia
   - ❑ a. found a notebook.
   - ❑ b. lost her notebook.

2. Mr. Wallace gave Georgia
   - ❑ a. a scolding.
   - ❑ b. the prize for the poetry contest.

3. After she won the contest, Georgia was
   - ❑ a. happy.
   - ❑ b. unhappy.

4. Georgia recognized the young man because his picture was in the
   - ❑ a. newspaper.
   - ❑ b. notebook.

5. Which is true?
   - ❑ a. The young man wrote the poem that won the contest.
   - ❑ b. Georgia wrote the poem that won the contest.

6. Why did Georgia mow the lawn?
   - ❑ a. Her parents told her to mow the lawn.
   - ❑ b. Georgia felt that she had done wrong.

Vocabulary

7. Georgia's talent surprised Mr. Wallace. To have *talent* means
   - ❑ a. you write many poems.
   - ❑ b. you can do something well.

8. You use the word *congratulations* to a tell a person that you are
   - ❑ a. not happy about something the person did.
   - ❑ b. happy when something good happened to the person.

9. Georgia realized that she knew the man's face. The word *realize* means
   - ❑ a. suddenly learn something.
   - ❑ b. make a drawing of something.

Idioms

10. The idiom *look forward to* means
   - ❑ a. get excited about what will happen in the future.
   - ❑ b. look directly ahead and not look at anything else.

How many questions did you answer correctly? Circle your score. Then fill in your score on the Score Chart on page 152.

Number Correct	1	2	3	4	5	6	7	8	9	10
Score	10	20	30	40	50	60	70	80	90	100

EXERCISES TO HELP YOU

Exercise A

Building sentences. Make sentences by adding the correct letter.

1. The notebook was _____
2. Georgia's poem _____
3. Mr. Wallace gave _____
4. Georgia received _____

    a. won first place.
    b. filled with drawings and poems.
    c. congratulations from her family and friends.
    d. Georgia a prize.

Now write the sentences on the lines below. Begin each sentence with a capital letter. End it with a period.

1. _____
2. _____
3. _____
4. _____

Now do numbers 5–8 the same way.

5. Georgia wasn't

    looking _____

6. Georgia recognized _____
7. The man said that _____
8. Georgia spent _____

    a. the young man.
    b. forward to summer.
    c. rest of the summer inside.
    d. Georgia chose one of his favorite poems.

5. _____
6. _____
7. _____
8. _____

Exercise B

Understanding the story. Answer each question. Write complete sentences. Look back at the story.

1. Where did Georgia go for lunch the day of the contest?

   <u>She went   </u>.

2. Georgia found a notebook. What was the notebook filled with?

   <u>It was   </u>.

3. What did Georgia receive from Mr. Wallace?

   <u>She received   </u>.

4. What did Georgia receive from her family and friends?

   <u>   </u>.

5. Who was mowing the lawn on the hot day?

   <u>   </u>.

6. How did Georgia recognize the young man?

   <u>His face   </u>.

7. What did the man tell Georgia?

   <u>He said she chose   </u>.

8. Where did Georgia spend the rest of the summer?

   <u>She spent   </u>.

Exercise C

Using the past tense. Retell the story. Write complete sentences. Use the past tense form of the verbs. Some verbs are regular. Some verbs are irregular. Follow the example.

Example:
Georgia /go home
Georgia went home for lunch.

1. Georgia / go to her favorite place

   _____.

2. Georgia/ notice a notebook

   _____.

3. She / read a poem

   _____.

4. Her poem / win first place

   _____.

5. Mr. Wallace / give her the prize

   _____.

6. Georgia / receive congratulations

   _____.

7. Georgia / be sad

   _____.

8. Georgia / hear a lawn mower

   _____.

9. Georgia / hand the man a glass of water

   _____.

10. The man / speak to Georgia

    _____.

11. Georgia / choose one of his favorite poems

    _____.

12. The man / walk out of view

    _____.

Exercise D
Adding an adjective. Complete the sentences by adding the correct adjective. Use each adjective once.

favorite

1. Georgia went to one of her _____ places for lunch.

happy

2. She got _____ in the faces in the notebook.

interested

3. On the _____ day of school, Georgia received the prize.

last

4. Georgia won the poetry contest, but she wasn't _____.

serious

5. One day the heat was _____. She heard the lawn mower.

terrible

6. The young man gave Georgia a _____ look. He knew that she used his favorite poem.

Exercise E

Adding vocabulary. On the left are five words and an idiom from the story. Complete each sentence by adding the correct word or words.

congratulations 1. Georgia won the poetry contest. Georgia's family was proud of her. Georgia received _____ from her family.

hesitated 2. Mr. Wallace said that Georgia's _____ surprised him. He didn't know she was so good at writing poetry.

hired 3. She was unhappy. She didn't _____ summer.

look forward to 4. Georgia's parents paid someone money to mow the lawn. They _____ someone to do the job.

realized 5. Georgia saw the man mowing the lawn. She _____ that his face was in the notebook.

talent 6. The young black man _____ and then he spoke. He offered Georgia congratulations about the poetry contest.

Exercise F

Speaking up. Look at the conversations. Practice them with a partner.

SHARING WITH OTHERS

Activity A

Taking a survey. Follow the directions.

1. What are your favorite things? Look at the chart. Complete the column under "You."
2. Now work with a partner. Ask your partner questions. Complete the right side of the chart.

Ask questions like this:
What is your favorite story in this book?
Who is your favorite person in this book?

	You	Your Partner
Favorite story in this book		
Favorite character in this book		
Favorite song		
Favorite poem		
Favorite movie		

Activity B

Sharing ideas. It's fun to share ideas with others. Discuss these questions with your partner or with the group. Write your answer to one of the questions.

The word *guilt* means to feel sorry that you did something wrong.
Why does Georgia feel guilt?

How did the poetry contest change Georgia's life? Why does Georgia mow the lawn?

When people do something wrong, sometimes they are punished. What was Georgia's punishment? Who gave her the punishment?

How do you feel about Georgia? Do you feel sorry for her? Why or why not?

Score Chart

This is the Score Chart for You Can Answer These Questions.
Shade in your score for each unit. For example, if your score
was 80 for **Hello, Good-bye,** look at the bottom of the chart for
Hello, Good-bye. Shade in the bar up to the 80 mark. By looking at this chart, you can see how well you did on each unit.

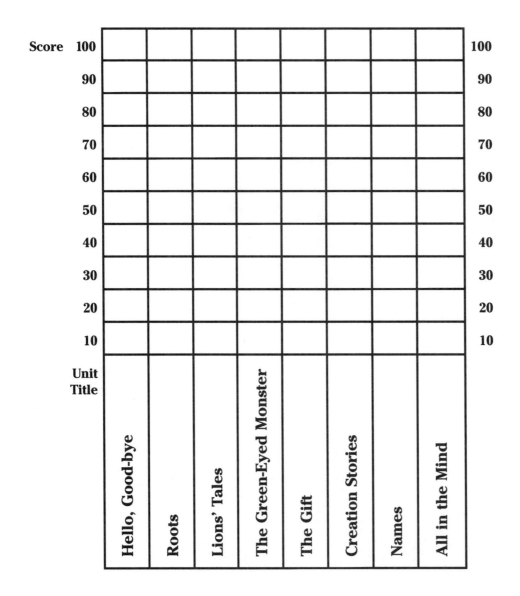

Score	100									100
	90									90
	80									80
	70									70
	60									60
	50									50
	40									40
	30									30
	20									20
	10									10
Unit Title		Hello, Good-bye	Roots	Lions' Tales	The Green-Eyed Monster	The Gift	Creation Stories	Names	All in the Mind	

	An Ancient Greek Hero	Sticks and Stones	The World is Wrong, Not Me	Apples, Apples	Harvest Time	Guilt and Grass, Part One	Guilt and Grass, Part Two
100							
90							
80							
70							
60							
50							
40							
30							
20							
10							